somatic YOGA
FOR BEGINNERS

Noah Schmitz

© Copyright 2024 by Noah Schmitz- All rights reserved.

This document is geared towards providing exact and reliable information in regard to the topic and issue covered. The publication is sold with the idea that the publisher is not required to render accounting, officially permitted, or otherwise, qualified services. If advice is necessary, legal or professional, a practiced individual in the profession should be ordered.

From a Declaration of Principles which was accepted and approved equally by a Committee of the American Bar Association and a Committee of Publishers and Associations. In no way is it legal to reproduce, duplicate, or transmit any part of this document in either electronic means or in printed format. Recording of this publication is strictly prohibited, and any storage of this document is not allowed unless with written permission from the publisher. All rights reserved.

The information provided herein is stated to be truthful and consistent, in that any liability, in terms of inattention or otherwise, by any usage or abuse of any policies, processes, or directions contained within is the solitary and utter responsibility of the recipient reader. Under no circumstances will any legal responsibility or blame be held against the publisher for any reparation, damages, or monetary loss due to the information herein, either directly or indirectly.

Respective authors own all copyrights not held by the publisher. The information herein is offered for informational purposes solely and is universal as such. The presentation of the information is without a contract or any type of guaranteed assurance. The trademarks that are used are without any consent, and the publication of the trademark is without permission or backing by the trademark owner. All trademarks and brands within this book are for clarifying purposes only and are owned by the owners themselves, not affiliated with this document.

Contents

Introduction	1
1. Starting Your Somatic Journey Understanding Somatic Therapy	3
2. Do Shorter Focus Sessions Really Work?	9
3. Somatic Breathing Work as a Foundation	14
4. Somatic Poses for Emotional Regulation	25
5. Somatic Poses for Stress and Tension Relief	42
6. Somatic Yoga for Strength and Flexibility	56
7. Somatic Yoga for Weight Loss	71
8. Your 21-Day Somatic Evolution	92
9. Your Future Using Somatic Yoga	102
Conclusion	114
Exercise List	118

Introduction

Yoga can appear to be deceptively simple to the casual observer. Someone who has glanced at a YouTube video might dismiss it as uneventful. However, those of us who practice yoga know better. Despite the slow, deliberate movements, a profound transformation is occurring within our bodies and minds.

In one moment, you're stretching toward your toes; in the next, you feel a satisfying crack in your back that lets you stand a little straighter. Changes in yoga might not always be instant, but they are impactful. It's important to note that not all yoga serves the same purpose. Some forms offer restorative benefits, while others might involve a vigorous 90-minute session in a heated room, aimed at detoxifying the body. And then there's *Somatic Yoga for Beginners*, a practice that extends beyond physical well-being to include emotional and mental health. Known as yoga "from the inside out," it's particularly suited for those who feel there aren't enough hours in the day. Life is hectic and often overwhelming. Somatic yoga, with its comprehensive approach, is an ideal solution for anyone struggling to find time for themselves in a busy schedule.

How can I speak so confidently about the benefits of somatic yoga? As a somatic yoga instructor, I've encountered numerous students, each facing their own unique struggles. However, a common thread connects them all: the stress of daily life and a lack of time for self-care. Time and again, I've witnessed the transformative effects of this practice. Just a few weeks of consistent somatic yoga can significantly improve our well-being.

In my experience, I've had the privilege to observe incredible changes in people's lives—relieving chronic pain, reducing anxiety, and fostering a deep sense of embodied wholeness. Somatic yoga has repeatedly demonstrated its efficacy as a powerful remedy for the complexities of contemporary life.

If you're seeking relief from your stressful life—and let's face it, who isn't?—somatic yoga might be the answer. Whether you aim to enhance your mind-body awareness for better focus at work, fully enjoy your life outside the office, or even lose weight through slow, low-impact movements, this practice offers a path to these benefits. Within this book, I'll explore how somatic yoga can help you achieve all of this and more.

Throughout this book, we'll uncover the fundamental principles and practices of somatic yoga. You'll gain the tools necessary to cultivate intense body awareness, learn strategies to release deep-seated tensions, and ultimately, reclaim your power and vitality. Exciting, isn't it?

So, let's begin this somatic yoga journey together. Your path to a healthier mental, physical, and emotional state begins now with the *"21-Day Transformative Journey to Unshakable Peace and Inner Healing."* Let's get started and unlock the full potential of your well-being!

Sounds good, right? Well, let's get started, then. The path to a healthy mental, physical, and emotional state awaits with your *21-Day Transformative Journey to Unshakable Peace and Inner Healing!*

Chapter One

Starting Your Somatic Journey

Understanding Somatic Therapy

Somatic Yoga is a holistic approach that deeply emphasizes the connection between mind and body. It draws on the principles of somatic psychology, various bodywork techniques, and traditional yoga practices to encourage practitioners to turn inward. This practice helps cultivate an acute awareness of bodily sensations, movements, and energetic flows. Unlike more physically intense yoga styles, Somatic Yoga features slow, gentle movements, focusing intently on proprioception—the natural ability to sense our body's position and movements. Enhancing this mind-body connection allows us to release deeply held tensions and relax stiff muscles, leading to a profound sense of complete, embodied wholeness.

These innovative approaches merged with the ancient wisdom of traditional yoga, lay the foundation for what we now recognize as Somatic Yoga. This practice seamlessly integrates the physical, emotional, and energetic dimensions, offering a profoundly transformative pathway to optimal health and vitality.

As we progress in our exploration of Somatic Yoga, remember that the objective is not to achieve the perfect pose or reach a lofty spiritual state. Instead, the focus is on cultivating a deep, enduring connection with the sacred wisdom of your own body. This connection opens the door to immense potential for healing, growth, and self-empowerment.

How Somatic Yoga Differs From Traditional Yoga Practices

To the untrained eye, the differences between various yoga styles may not be immediately obvious, yet they are quite significant for practitioners. So, how does Somatic Yoga stand apart from more traditional yoga practices?

Philosophically, Somatic Yoga represents a significant shift. Traditional yoga often focuses on achieving specific poses, mastering advanced techniques, and pursuing high spiritual objectives. In contrast, Somatic Yoga is founded on the principle that true transformation stems from an intimate understanding of our inner selves rather than external achievements. It encourages an individualized approach, inviting each practitioner to actively engage in their own healing and growth. The emphasis is not on perfecting a pose but on developing a deep awareness of bodily sensations, movements, and energetic flows. This approach, rooted in somatic psychology, facilitates experiential learning that can lead to profound personal insights and enhance our natural capacity for self-regulation.

This philosophical shift significantly influences how we approach asanas or yoga poses. In traditional yoga, the emphasis is typically on the external appearance of the pose, with practitioners working to align their bodies according to precise anatomical cues and striving for a picture-perfect expression. In contrast, Somatic Yoga encourages a deeper engagement with the subtle, internal sensations experienced within the body. Instead of conforming to predetermined shapes, we are taught to heed the intuitive wisdom of our own physical form, respecting its unique anatomical variations and the current limits of our flexibility and strength.

Through slow, mindful movements and a deep connection with our bodies, we cultivate a profound understanding of our structural and functional patterns. This empowers us to relieve areas of tension and promote greater ease and fluidity throughout the body. Let's explore how these approaches to yoga differ in more detail.

Somatic Yoga prioritizes internal sensations and the felt experience of the body in motion. Practitioners are encouraged to focus on subtle movements and varying tensions within their bodies. These movements are intentionally slower and more deliberate, enhancing practitioners' ability to interpret their bodies' feedback and adjust accordingly. In this context, asanas are viewed not just as physical postures but as opportunities to deepen the connection between mind and body.

In contrast, traditional yoga often emphasizes achieving precise external alignments in asanas, such as specific positioning of the feet, shoulders, or hips. The goal here is typically to conform to a predetermined shape or form. This approach can lead practitioners to prioritize external alignment over internal cues, sometimes at the expense of comfort or by ignoring bodily signals of discomfort.

While alignment remains important in Somatic Yoga, the approach is inherently more flexible and adaptable. It recognizes that optimal alignment may differ from one person to another, influenced by individual anatomy, past injuries, and other personal factors. This understanding allows Somatic Yoga to support a more personalized and responsive yoga practice.

There is a notable difference in dynamics between traditional yoga and Somatic Yoga. Somatic Yoga often emphasizes dynamic exploration within asanas, encouraging practitioners to move in and out of postures with fluidity and experiment with variations to discover what feels most comfortable for their bodies. In contrast, traditional yoga typically involves holding static asanas for extended periods, with a greater focus on maintaining the posture through steady breathing and concentrated focus. In Somatic Yoga, asanas are viewed as dynamic rather than fixed forms, allowing for adjustments throughout the practice.

In essence, Somatic Yoga liberates us from external expectations and rigid doctrines, opening a pathway to self-discovery and self-empowerment. This approach invites each individual to explore their unique physical and emotional landscapes, fostering a deep, personal connection with their practice.

The Importance of Body-Mind Connection in Somatic Yoga

The mind-body connection—the intricate interplay between our physical, emotional, and energetic states—is the cornerstone of holistic well-being and profound personal growth.

In our Western culture, which often prioritizes the intellect, we have become too accustomed to compartmentalizing ourselves—viewing the body as a separate entity to be managed, controlled, or even neglected. However, the reality is that our physical sensations, movements, and energetic patterns are deeply intertwined with our thoughts, emotions, and even our most profound subconscious beliefs.

When we practice Somatic Yoga, we move away from a fragmented view of ourselves and develop a deeper appreciation for how our mind and body function as a cohesive unit. You may have noticed this integration firsthand—the moment a persistent tension in your shoulders dissolves as you consciously breathe into that area, or the feeling of your heart rate slowing and a deep calm enveloping you as you ease into a restorative pose. These experiences are vivid demonstrations of the mind-body connection at work, showing that by honoring our body's wisdom, we can significantly affect our emotional, mental, and even spiritual health.

This is why the mind-body connection is fundamental to Somatic Yoga. By tuning into our bodily sensations and movements, we not only release chronic tensions but also reclaim our inherent abilities for self-regulation and healing. This journey of self-discovery can profoundly transform every facet of our lives, influencing how we engage in relationships and present ourselves to the world.

Therefore, as we proceed, keep the mind-body connection central to your awareness. It is within the sacred space of your own physical form that the true essence and transformative power of this practice begin to manifest. When we engage in Somatic Yoga, we take a step back from this fragmented perspective and instead grow this understanding of the ways in which our mind and body operate as an integrated whole. Perhaps you've experienced this firsthand—that moment when a deep, nagging tension in your shoulders suddenly melts away as you shift your focus and breathe into the area with intention. Or the sensation of your heart rate slowing, your breath deepening, and a profound sense of calm washing over you as you transition into a restorative pose. These are tangible demonstrations of the mind-body connection in action—proof that by honoring the wisdom of our physical bodies, we can profoundly influence our emotional, mental, and even spiritual well-being.

And this is precisely why the mind-body connection is so central to Somatic Yoga practice. By bringing awareness to our bodily sensations and movements, we release chronic tensions and, ultimately, reclaim our innate capacity for self-regulation and self-healing. It's a path to self-discovery that has the power to transform every aspect of our lives, from the way we navigate our relationships to the way we show up in the world.

So, as we move forward, keep the mind-body connection at the forefront of your awareness. For it is here, in the sacred sanctuary of your own physical forms, that the true magic of this practice truly begins to unfold.

One of the truly remarkable aspects of Somatic Yoga is its seamless integration of mindfulness—this act of being fully present that can profoundly transform our lives. As we delve deeper into this holistic practice, it becomes apparent that physical movements and postures are just components of a larger picture. Central to the Somatic Yoga experience is a sustained focus on tuning into the sensations, emotions, and thought patterns that emerge during practice.

Somatic Yoga utilizes guided meditations, breath-work exercises, and a strong emphasis on interoceptive awareness to help practitioners quiet the mind's chatter and turn their focus inward. Each slow, mindful movement invites us to become deeply aware of the ebb and flow of sensations—the tension in our shoulders, the subtle shifts in our balance, the gentle rhythm of our breathing. Instead of mechanically moving through poses, challenge yourself to deeply engage, listen, and let the practice uncover the profound layers of your being. In this sacred space of mindful awareness, the transformative power of Somatic Yoga truly begins to strengthen your mind, body, and soul.

The Benefits of Practicing Somatic Yoga

Let's get into the transformative benefits of practicing somatic yoga, as its rewards extend far beyond mere physical fitness.

Beginning with the physical advantages, Somatic Yoga employs slow, mindful movements and a deep emphasis on body awareness to enhance overall flexibility, strength, and postural alignment. However, its benefits extend further. Extensive research (Zilih, 2023) has demonstrated the profound impact of Somatic Yoga on mental and emotional well-being. By incorporating mindfulness techniques and nurturing a profound mind-body connection, this practice has been associated with reduced stress and anxiety, improved emotional regulation, and heightened self-awareness.

Stepping onto the Somatic Yoga mat isn't solely about physical exercise. Through mindful movement and embodied presence, we invite a sense of unity and wholeness that permeates not only our bodies but also our lives. These benefits aren't exclusive to experienced yogis. In fact, Somatic Yoga is particularly accessible for beginners, offering a gentle pathway to unlocking our innate capacities for self-regulation and self-healing.

So far, we've established that Somatic Yoga is a holistic practice deeply focused on the mind-body connection. Drawing from somatic psychology and traditional yoga, this approach encourages us to turn inward, enhance our body awareness, and tap into the profound potential for self-regulation and self-healing within us. We've seen how Somatic Yoga distinguishes itself from more conventional yoga practices through its emphasis on experiential learning, subtle movements, and respect for each practitioner's unique needs and abilities. By moving away from rigid expectations and dogma, we open ourselves to a truly transformative journey of self-discovery.

Furthermore, we've delved into the essential role that mindfulness plays in the Somatic Yoga experience. Through integrating breathwork and guided meditations, we can alleviate stress and anxiety while achieving a heightened sense of embodied wholeness.

Looking ahead to the next chapter, we will explore the power of shorter focus sessions, a distinctive aspect of Somatic Yoga. These sessions are designed to help us weave these transformative principles into our daily lives, even during our busiest days. By dedicating just a few moments to mindful movement and presence, we'll learn how to maintain balance, resilience, and self-care, no matter the challenges life throws our way.

Chapter Two

Do Shorter Focus Sessions Really Work?

Now that we've explored the foundations of Somatic Yoga and its transformative power, let's discuss how we can integrate this practice into our daily lives through short focus sessions.

While we might wish to allocate large chunks of time to our self-care rituals, the reality of today's fast-paced, high-demand world often makes long yoga sessions or extended meditation practices feel more like chores on an already crowded to-do list. Research indicates that prolonged periods of cognitive focus can lead to fatigue, boredom, and a gradual loss of interest—exactly what we aim to avoid in a holistic wellness routine (Kok, 2022).

This is precisely where the value of shorter focus sessions comes in. By distilling our Somatic Yoga practice into manageable, incremental segments, we can accomplish more with less. Instead of enduring lengthy sessions that can seem daunting, we can access the benefits of this practice in just a few precious moments throughout our day. Imagine taking a quick 5–10-minute break from your desk to tune into the subtle sensations in your body, releasing tension with mindful movements and deep, nourishing breaths. Or spending just 15 minutes each morning moving intentionally, expanding your awareness before plunging into the day's tasks. These brief yet potent sessions of presence and self-care can yield substantial benefits, both immediately and over time.

The beauty of shorter focus sessions lies in their adaptability to the natural rhythms and constraints of our daily lives. These sessions allow us to meet ourselves exactly where we are, enabling the development of a sustainable Somatic Yoga practice that blends seamlessly into our routines. This approach facilitates a gradual transformation of our mindsets and behaviors from the inside out, enhancing our overall well-being without overwhelming us.

The Benefits of Short Somatic Yoga Workouts

One of the standout features of Somatic Yoga is its ability to yield remarkable results within a concise timeframe. Compared to more traditional yoga routines that can be quite time-consuming, the short, targeted sessions characteristic of Somatic Yoga are designed to quickly engage the mind-body connection and deliver all its associated benefits. These sessions are not only effective but also highly accessible.

Recent research underscores that consistency in practice is often more crucial than the length of each session for achieving enduring benefits in both physical and mental health (Stoewen, 2017). By participating in these brief, focused sessions regularly, you'll not only enjoy immediate relaxation and ease, but you'll also witness long-term improvements in stress resilience, emotional regulation, and overall well-being.

Ways to Integrate Daily Routines for Busy People

As I've pointed out, one of the most crucial things about short focus sessions is just how seamlessly they can be integrated into our daily routine. Let me give you a few scenarios starting with integrating this practice in the mornings.

Imagine taking just 10-15 minutes to greet the day with a gentle, mindful Somatic Yoga sequence. Perhaps you begin by tuning into your breath, allowing it to anchor you in the present moment. From there, you might move through a series of slow, deliberate movements—gently opening the hips and releasing tension in the shoulders. By starting your day in this way, you're not only awakening the physical form but also setting the tone for a heightened state of mental clarity and emotional balance throughout the day. And of course, all of this can be done right from the comfort of your own home, requiring no special equipment or extensive preparation.

Now, let's talk about midday—that time when our energy levels can start to wane and our focus begins to falter. This is the perfect opportunity to weave in a quick Somatic Yoga break, whether it's a 10-minute sequence at your desk or a brief stroll around the block, moving with intention and presence. You can tune inward and release pent-up tension. You'll find that you're able to return to your tasks with renewed vigor, sharper focus, and a greater sense of calmness.

And as the sun sets and the day winds down, Somatic Yoga can once again become a powerful ally in your self-care toolkit. Perhaps with only 10 or 15 minutes in the evening to slowly flow through gentle postures. Or maybe you simply take a few moments to sit in quiet meditation, attuned to the subtle rhythms of your body, and letting go of any lingering stresses or worries.

The beauty of these shorter focus sessions is in their sheer versatility. By incorporating them seamlessly into your daily life, you're not only investing in your physical well-being, but also nurturing your mental, emotional, and even spiritual resilience. And when you consider that just 10 minutes of Somatic Yoga practice is equivalent to 20 minutes of effective work toward your holistic healing, the potential becomes truly awe-inspiring.

Strategies for Incorporating Somatic Yoga Into Your Busy Life

I understand that while everything sounds good on paper, there are still some things that you need to be aware of when incorporating Somatic yoga exercises into your routine. And because of that, let's look into some truly practical tips and strategies so you can incorporate them into even the busiest of schedules. Because trust me, with a little creativity and dedication, the opportunities are endless!

First and foremost, I want to emphasize the importance of prioritizing your self-care and mindfulness practices, even amidst the whirlwind of daily life. I know it can be tempting to push these things to the side, especially when there are a million other demands on our time and energy. But the truth is, investing in your own well-being is one of the most powerful things you can do, both for yourself and for the people in your life.

So, start by identifying those small pockets of time in your day—maybe it's first thing in the morning, during your lunch break, or right before bed—and commit to even just 10–15 minutes to devote to your Somatic Yoga practice. And remember, flexibility is key. If your schedule shifts unexpectedly or you find yourself with an extra 5 minutes to spare, don't be afraid to adapt and get creative. I can't emphasize enough just how seamlessly these exercises can be integrated into the rhythms of our daily lives. Perhaps you find yourself mindfully flowing through a few gentle postures while waiting for the coffee to brew or taking a few moments to tune into your breath during a transition between tasks. By adding these incremental acts of self-care throughout your day, you'll start to notice a profound shift in your overall sense of embodiment, emotional regulation, and resilience.

And don't forget, you can also get incredibly creative with your Somatic Yoga practice by incorporating it into your daily activities. Maybe you take a mindful walking break around the block, or you practice a few centered, grounding movements while folding the laundry. The possibilities are truly endless, and the key is to find what works best for you and your unique lifestyle.

Setting Realistic Expectations

I believe it's important that we take a moment to talk about realistic expectations before beginning with Somatic Yoga exercises. This journey of self-discovery and change is not about achieving some lofty, picture-perfect state of being. It's about the process, the gradual unfolding, and the willingness to embrace where we are, right here and now.

I'll talk more about the concept of "progress over perfection" later on in the book, but for now, let's just focus on the importance of celebrating those small wins. We need to remember to be patient as we go through this initial phase. Progress in Somatic Yoga is often not linear. Some days, you may feel like everything is going nice and easy, while others, well, not so much. But that's okay, it's part of the journey. What you need to remember is that consistency in practice is the way forward.

The key is to approach each moment, each practice, with a beginner's mind. Recognize that your body and your needs will shift and evolve, and be willing to adapt and modify your approach accordingly. Because when we release the need for perfection and instead embrace the messy, beautiful process of self-discovery, that's when we know we're heading in the right direction.

Before we move forward to the next chapter, I want to emphasize the effectiveness of short focus sessions, as these are a big part of Somatic Yoga. Incremental practices offer a remarkably efficient and accessible way to reap the profound benefits of Somatic Yoga, even for those of us who are constantly busy. Take out just 10, 15, or 20 minutes throughout your day to enhance your physical well-being and improve your emotional regulation. We also discussed the crucial role that consistency plays in our journey toward holistic transformation. Rather than forcing ourselves to endure lengthy, daunting yoga sessions, we discovered how the cumulative effects of these short, focused practices can catalyze incredible shifts in our overall health and vitality.

In the next chapter, we'll be going through the foundational role of Somatic Breathwork—a powerful practice that, when combined with the principles of shorter focus sessions, has the potential to unlock even deeper levels of embodiment, emotional resilience, and personal transformation.

Chapter Three

Somatic Breathing Work as a Foundation

Now that we have covered the fundamentals of somatic yoga and the importance of short focus sessions, it's time to discuss another important aspect—Somatic Breathing. Breathing is the fuel that powers Somatic Yoga. For centuries, various traditions and modalities, from ancient yoga and meditation practices to modern somatic therapies, have recognized the profound influence that our breath has on us, from our physical to our emotional and energetic well-being.

In fact, the roots of Somatic Breathwork can be traced back to the pioneering work of early 20th-century practitioners, such as Wilhelm Reich and Ida Rolf, who recognized the intricate connections between our respiratory patterns, the state of our nervous system, and the way we experience and process emotions (Jacobson, 2011). These visionaries understood that, by intentionally working with the breath, we could find self-regulation, release deeply held tensions, and ultimately reclaim our innate capacity for healing and growth.

Understanding this will make your integration into Somatic Yoga a lot easier (not that it's hard, as you might have guessed by now). Instead of treating breathwork as a separate practice, we incorporate it into our movement sequences, using the rhythmic flow of inhalation and exhalation to guide and inform our every action.

The Importance of Breath Awareness in Somatic Yoga

The breath is an incredible bridge that connects all our states. With each inhalation and exhalation, we're not only oxygenating our bodies and regulating our autonomic nervous system, but we're also influencing the way we experience and process our thoughts and feelings. Research has shown, for instance, that conscious breathwork can have a marked impact on our stress and anxiety levels, helping to calm the mind, soothe the nervous system, and facilitate a state of deep relaxation (Zaccaro et al., 2018). And when we bring this heightened breath awareness into our Somatic Yoga practice, we increase the mind-body integration levels.

But there's more to it than just breathing exercises. With each moment we pause to tune into the subtle sensations of our inhalations and exhalations, we anchor ourselves firmly in the present moment, creating our own space to observe our inner experience with clarity and compassion.

Techniques for Deepening the Breath and Calming the Nervous System

Now that we know how important breathing is, let's get to some actual techniques, shall we?

Diaphragmatic breathing, also known as belly breathing, is an essential practice. You have to draw the breath deep into the abdomen, which allows your diaphragm to expand and contract.

To start, just find a comfortable seated or lying position, then, place one hand on your belly, just below the navel. As you inhale, you can feel your belly gently rise and expand, allowing the air to fill the lower lobes of your lungs. Then, as you exhale, let your belly soften and release, creating a natural contraction of the diaphragm.

A study has proved that this type of deep, slow breathing can have a profound impact on our physiological and emotional states, activating the parasympathetic nervous system and promoting feelings of calm and relaxation (Gerritsen & Band, 2018).

Another powerful breath technique to explore is extended exhalation. By consciously lengthening the duration of our exhales, we can effectively override the body's stress response, allowing the mind to settle and the nervous system to find a state of balance and equilibrium.

Simply begin by taking a normal inhalation, and then slowly and gently extend the exhalation, feeling the airflow out of your body. You might even try counting to four or six on the inhale and then extending the exhale to a count of six or eight. With practice, you can gradually increase the ratio of exhalation to inhalation, ushering in profound states of relaxation and clarity.

And finally, one of my personal favorites: alternate nostril breathing, or Nadi Shodhana in the yogic tradition. This balancing practice involves closing off one nostril at a time, allowing you to consciously direct the flow of air and harmonize the two hemispheres of your brain.

Use your right thumb to gently close off your right nostril, and then inhale slowly through the left nostril. At the top of the inhalation, close off the left nostril with your right ring finger and exhale through the right nostril. Continue alternating the nostrils with each cycle of breath, allowing this intentional practice to quiet the mind and restore a sense of emotional and energetic equilibrium.

Somatic Breathing Exercises for Relaxation and Stress Relief

Let's now look at some other types of exercises, in this case for relaxation and stress relief.

Box Breathing

- Begin by finding a comfortable seated or lying position, and allow your eyes to gently close.

- As you inhale, visualize drawing the breath down into your belly, feeling it expand like a balloon.

- Hold your breath for a moment at the top of the inhale, then exhale slowly, allowing your belly to soften and release.

- Continue this pattern, inhaling for a count of four, holding for four, exhaling for four, and holding again for four.

- As you move through the cycles, take a moment to tune into any areas of tension or discomfort in your body and consciously release them with each exhale.

Using this structured breathing technique has been shown to have an impact on our heart rate, stress levels, and emotional and physiological regulation (Pal & Velkumary, 2004).

3-Part Breath or Dirga Pranayama

- Start by inhaling slowly, first filling the lower belly, then the rib cage, and finally the upper chest.

- Pause briefly at the top of the inhalation, then exhale fully, allowing the breath to flow out from the upper chest, down through the rib cage, and out through the belly.

This expansive, multi-dimensional breathing pattern helps to oxygenate the body, calm the mind, and promote a profound sense of embodied presence.

Ocean Breath or Ujjayi Pranayama

- Start by inhaling and exhaling through the nose

- Gently begin constricting the back of the throat to create a soft, ocean-like sound.

- As you continue to breathe, you may notice a deepening of your focus, a calming of the mind, and an overall sense of internal harmony.

This technique is particularly helpful for promoting parasympathetic nervous system activation, which can help to lower stress, ease anxiety, and facilitate a state of deep relaxation (Kaushik et al., 2005). And when practiced in conjunction with mindful movement and somatic awareness, the benefits can be truly remarkable.

Cultivating Breath Awareness in Daily Life

Breath is remarkably accessible and versatile. No matter where we are or what we're doing, we can always turn our attention inward and use the rhythm of our inhalations and exhalations as a means of bringing mindfulness and presence. Maybe you'll find yourself stuck in traffic or waiting in a long line. Instead of letting the frustration rise, take a moment to tune into your breath. Feel the air moving in and out, allowing each exhale to release any tension or stress you may be holding. Or maybe you're sitting at your desk, feeling your focus start to waver. Here, just pause, take a few deep, nourishing breaths, and let the weight of the world melt away, even if just for a moment. Breathing is easy, like that.

You can add "breathing breaks" throughout your day. Simply set a timer on your phone, or listen to the cues of your body, and take a few minutes to drop into a state of deep, mindful breathing. Remember that intentional breathing can serve as an ever-present anchor, a reliable touchstone that you can return to whenever life starts to feel overwhelming. When the demands of the world seem to be crashing in or when you find yourself lost in a whirlwind of anxious thoughts, simply turn your attention inward and connect with the steady rhythm of your inhalations and exhalations.

As we've seen, the breath serves as the very foundation upon which this holistic practice is built. Through the cultivation of mindful breathing techniques, we can dive into profound physiological and emotional regulation, calming the nervous system, reducing stress and anxiety, and promoting a profound sense of embodied presence and self-awareness. And when we intertwine these breathwork practices seamlessly into our Somatic Yoga sequences, the benefits are immense. Whether it's the grounding, restorative power of Box Breathing, the expansive, oxygenating qualities of the 3-Part Breath, or the soothing, meditative essence of Ocean Breath, each technique offers a unique pathway towards greater relaxation and emotional balance.

Warming Up With Breath

Warm-up stretches are vitally important to prepare your body for your somatic yoga practice and to properly synchronize your breath with each of your movements.

The warm-up stretches below can be used as a stand-alone practice to help calm your body and mind during the day, or as powerful warm-up stretches before you begin your somatic yoga routine.

Select a breathwork exercise above, and try to stretch while using your breath.

Deep Hip Stretch

- Begin in a high plank position with your hands shoulder-width apart and your wrists directly under your shoulders.

- Your body should form a straight line from your head to your heels, engaging your core muscles to maintain stability.

- Lift your right foot off the ground and bring it forward to the outside of your right hand.

- Place your foot flat on the ground with your toes pointing slightly outward.

- Keep your left leg extended straight back behind you.

- Ensure your right knee is stacked directly above your right ankle, forming a 90-degree angle.

- Lower your hips toward the ground, sinking into the stretch.

- You should feel a deep stretch in your left hip flexor and groin area.

- Hold the stretch for up to 8 breath counts.

- Focus on relaxing into the stretch and feeling the tension release in your hips and groin.

- Repeat the same steps on the other side, bringing your left foot forward outside your left hand.

Supine Glute Stretch

- Begin by lying on your back on a comfortable surface, such as a yoga mat, with both knees bent and feet flat on the floor.

- Extend your right leg straight out in front of you, keeping your left knee bent with your foot flat on the floor.

- Cross your right ankle over your left knee, creating a figure-four shape with your legs.

- Reach your hands around your left thigh or shin and gently pull your left knee towards your chest until you feel a stretch in your right glute and outer hip.

- Keep your head and shoulders relaxed on the ground, allowing your lower back to settle into the mat.

- Hold the stretch for 8 breath counts.

- Repeat the stretch on the other side by switching legs.

Reverse Lunge Reach

- Begin standing tall with your feet hip-width apart and your arms at your sides.

- Take a step back with your right foot, lowering your body into a reverse lunge position.

- As you lower into the lunge, simultaneously reach both arms overhead, extending through your fingertips.

- Keep your left knee aligned with your left ankle, forming a 90-degree angle, while your right knee hovers just above the ground.

- Engage your core muscles to maintain balance and stability throughout the movement.

- Feel a stretch through the front of your right hip and thigh as you reach your arms upward.

- Hold the lunge position for up to 8 breath counts.

- Return to the starting position by pushing through your left heel and bringing your right foot back to meet your left foot.

- Repeat the movement on the other side.

Deep Neck Stretch

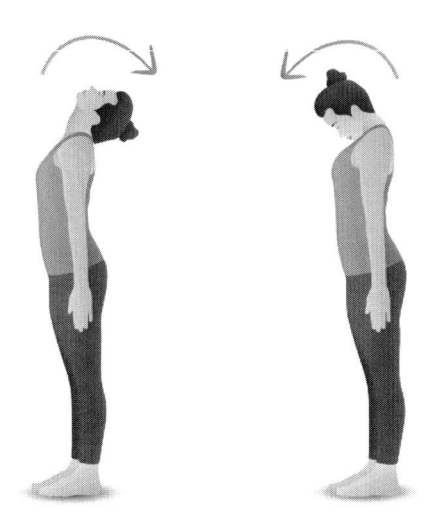

- Start in a comfortable seated or standing position with your spine tall and shoulders relaxed.

- Inhale deeply, then as you exhale, slowly tilt your head forward, bringing your chin towards your chest.

- Hold this position for 4 breath counts, feeling a gentle stretch along the back of your neck.

- Inhale again, then exhale as you slowly lift your head back to the center.

- Now, inhale and gently tilt your head backward, looking up towards the ceiling.

- Hold for another 4 breath counts, feeling a stretch along the front of your neck.

- Inhale once more, then exhale as you bring your head back to the center.

Kneeling Turn and Reach

You have the video example

- Start by kneeling on the floor with your knees hip-width apart and your toes pointing behind you.

- Engage your core muscles to stabilize your torso and maintain an upright posture.

- Extend your right arm out to the side at shoulder height, palm facing down.

- Inhale deeply, then exhale as you rotate your torso to the left, reaching your right arm across your body towards the left side.

- Keep your hips facing forward as you twist, feeling a stretch through your spine and the muscles along your right side.

- Hold the stretch for 10 breath counts.

- Inhale again, then exhale as you slowly return to the starting position, bringing your right arm back to shoulder height.

- Repeat the movement on the other side, extending your left arm out to the side and rotating your torso to the right.

As we proceed, I encourage you to continue exploring and experimenting with these transformative Somatic Breathing exercises. Incorporate them into your daily life, use them as tools for self-regulation and self-care, and allow them to be your constant companions on this incredible journey of embodiment and personal growth. And speaking of which, in our next chapter, we'll be exploring the myriad ways in which specific poses and movement sequences can be leveraged to promote emotional regulation, unlock areas of energetic and psychological blockage, and ultimately catalyze profound shifts in our overall well-being.

Chapter Four

Somatic Poses for Emotional Regulation

In this chapter, we're going to explore the connection between our physical body and our emotions and the critical importance of emotional regulation. As we explore more of the somatic yoga practice, we will learn to grow emotional well-being and it will be a central theme here.

When we become emotionally dysregulated—whether it's overwhelming feelings of stress, anxiety, anger, or even depression—the effects can cascade throughout our entire being. Physiologically, emotional dysregulation triggers the release of stress hormones like cortisol, which can compromise our immune system, disrupt our sleep, and even contribute to chronic pain and illness over time. Emotionally, when we lose the ability to manage our feelings in a healthy, constructive way, it becomes increasingly difficult to navigate life's challenges. We could lose our temper with family members, find it difficult to focus at work, or even become mired in negative thoughts that further exacerbate the issue.

The good news is that we can regain our ability to control our emotions through the practice of Somatic Yoga. According to a study, breathing exercises can really help reset our autonomic nervous system, which calms the "fight-or-flight" reaction and enables us to handle stress more composedly, for instance (Porges, 2011). The strategies we'll study can also help us identify the underlying causes of our emotional imbalances and take the necessary steps to heal them from the inside out. In the end, our whole well-being ultimately rests on our capacity to control our emotions. Our ability to handle life's ups and downs with adaptability, clarity, and inner resourcefulness allows us to experience a deep feeling of resilience and freedom.

Exploring the Connection Between Emotions and Physical Tension

The connection between emotions and physical tension is a vital aspect of Somatic Yoga, as it helps us understand how our inner emotional self directly impacts our bodily experience. At the core of the mind-body connection is the simple yet profound truth that we don't just think about our emotions; we actually feel them in our physical form. When we experience a strong emotional response, whether it's anxiety, anger, or grief, our bodies instinctively react. We might clench our jaw, tighten our shoulders, or feel a knotting sensation in the pit of our stomach.

The way we hold tension in our physical body can also inform and influence our emotional state. This can be backed by a study that found that simply adopting a slouched, contracted posture can trigger feelings of low self-worth and depression, while an upright, open posture can boost confidence and a positive mood (Peper & Lin, 2012). This is particularly evident when it comes to the debilitating effects of chronic stress. As the body remains in a perpetual state of high alertness, the musculature becomes increasingly rigid and constricted. This not only contributes to physical symptoms like headaches and back pain but also has a profound impact on our emotional well-being (Charmandari et al., 2005). Yet another research has shown that individuals dealing with high levels of stress often exhibit poor emotional regulation, experiencing more frequent and intense negative emotions. The inability to effectively manage these feelings can then further exacerbate the physiological stress response, creating a vicious cycle that takes a heavy toll on our overall health and quality of life (Gross & Muñoz, 1995).

Moreover, the neurochemical imbalances caused by prolonged stress can significantly impact our mood and emotional regulation as research has shown. Here, specialists found that chronic stress can lead to a depletion of neurotransmitters like serotonin and dopamine, which play crucial roles in regulating our emotions and promoting feelings of well-being and happiness (Pizzagalli, 2014). As a result, we may find ourselves more prone to mood disturbances like irritability, sadness, and even depression.

This emotional dysregulation can make it increasingly challenging to navigate life's ups and downs with composure and grace. We may find ourselves overreacting to minor stressors, struggling to maintain healthy relationships, or feeling a pervasive sense of emotional exhaustion and burnout. Over time, this chronic emotional strain can erode our sense of self-worth, leading to patterns of negative self-talk and self-judgment that further perpetuate the cycle of stress and suffering. It's important to recognize that these emotional impacts of stress are not a sign of personal weakness or failure but rather a natural consequence of our body's adaptive response to perceived threats. So, by acknowledging the link between our stress levels and our emotional well-being, we can begin to approach ourselves with greater compassion and understanding and seek out practices and support systems that promote healing from these negative aspects in our lives. By understanding this intimate mind-body connection, you can acquire a powerful tool for fostering emotional balance and resilience.

Somatic Yoga Poses to Release Emotional Blockages and Promote Emotional Balance

Forward Fold (Uttanasana)

- Start in a standing position at the top of your mat with your feet hip-width apart, arms by your sides, and spine tall.

- Take a deep breath in, engaging your core and lengthening your spine.

- As you exhale, slowly begin to hinge forward at your hips, leading with your chest and keeping your back flat.

- Continue to fold forward, allowing your hands to come down towards the floor. You can bend your knees slightly if needed to maintain a straight spine.

- Once you reach your maximum forward fold, allow your upper body to relax completely, letting your head hang heavy towards the floor.

- If your hands don't reach the floor, you can place them on your shins, and ankles, or use yoga blocks for support.

- Keep your weight evenly distributed between your feet, with a slight shift towards the balls of your feet.

- Relax your neck and shoulders, allowing any tension to melt away.

- Take several deep breaths in this pose, focusing on lengthening your spine with each inhale and deepening the stretch with each exhale.

- Hold the pose for 30 seconds to 1 minute, or longer if comfortable.

- To release the pose, engage your core muscles and slowly begin to roll up to standing, stacking one vertebra on top of the other.

- Once you are fully upright, take a moment to pause and notice any sensations in your body.

Child's Pose (Balasana)

- Start in a kneeling position on your mat with your knees hip-width apart and your big toes touching behind you.

- Sit back on your heels, allowing your hips to sink towards your heels.

- Take a deep breath in and lengthen your spine, reaching your arms overhead.

- As you exhale, slowly begin to hinge forward at your hips, lowering your torso towards the mat.

- Extend your arms forward and lower your chest towards the floor, resting your forehead on the mat.

- Allow your arms to reach out in front of you, palms facing down, or if it's more comfortable, you can bring your arms alongside your body with your palms facing up.

- Keep your knees hip-width apart or wider, depending on your comfort level. You can also bring your knees together if that feels better for your body.

- Relax your shoulders, neck, and jaw, letting go of any tension.

- Take slow, deep breaths in this pose, allowing your belly to expand with each inhale and releasing any tension with each exhale.

- Hold Child's Pose for 1 minute, or as long as it feels comfortable for you.

- To release the pose, gently walk your hands back towards your body, lifting your torso upright. You can sit back on your heels for a moment before coming to a comfortable seated position.

Heart-Opening Pose

- Start on your hands and knees with your wrists directly under your shoulders and your knees directly under your hips.

- Spread your fingers wide and press firmly into the mat with your palms.

- Slowly walk your hands forward, extending your arms out in front of you while keeping your hips directly over your knees.

- Allow your chest to descend towards the floor.

- Continue to walk your hands forward until your chest reaches or hovers just above the mat.

- Keep your arms active and engaged, with your elbows lifted slightly off the ground.

- If it feels comfortable for your neck, gently lower your forehead to the mat.

- Alternatively, you can keep your forehead hovering above the ground or rest it on a yoga block or folded blanket for support.

- Lengthen your spine from your tailbone to the crown of your head, creating space between each vertebra.

- Avoid collapsing into your lower back; instead, engage your core muscles to support your spine.

- Stay in the Heart-Opening Pose for 30 seconds.

Cat-Cow Pose (Marjaryasana-Bitilasana)

- Begin on your hands and knees with your wrists directly under your shoulders and your knees directly under your hips.

- Spread your fingers wide and press firmly into the mat with your palms.

- Keep your spine neutral, with your head in line with your spine.

- As you inhale, arch your back and tilt your pelvis down toward the floor, allowing your belly to sink toward the mat.

- Lift your chest and gaze forward, creating a gentle arch in your lower back.

- Lift your tailbone towards the ceiling and broaden across your collarbones. Imagine lengthening your spine from your tailbone to the crown of your head.

- As you exhale, round your back and tuck your chin towards your chest, like a cat stretching its spine.

- Press into your palms and draw your belly button towards your spine, engaging your core muscles.

- Drop your head towards the floor and feel a stretch across your upper back and between your shoulder blades.

- Allow your shoulder blades to spread apart and feel the space between them.

- Inhale as you transition back into Cow Pose, arching your back and lifting your chest, and gaze forward.

- Exhale as you transition into Cat Pose, rounding your back and tucking your chin towards your chest.

- Continue to flow smoothly between Cat and Cow, syncing your movements with your breath.

- Allow the rhythm of your breath to guide your movements, creating a fluid and meditative flow.

- Continue to move through the Cat-Cow sequence for 5 to 10 breath cycles, or as many times as feels comfortable for you.

Pigeon Pose (Eka Pada Rajakapotasana)

- Begin in a seated position hands shoulder-width apart and your feet hip-width apart.

- Inhale and bend your right leg in front of you as you slowly straighten your left leg behind you.

- Extend your left leg straight back behind you, if possible, keeping your hips squared towards the front of your mat.

- Point your left toes and press the top of your left foot into the mat.

- Check that your hips are squared towards the front of your mat, with your right hip pointing towards the mat and your left hip lifting slightly.

- This alignment helps to deepen the stretch in the hip flexors and quadriceps.

- To release this pose, inhale to lengthen your spine, then exhale and slowly lower your upper body towards the mat.

- Press into your hands and lift your chest up.

- Slide your left leg back to its starting position.

- Hold this pose for 30 seconds, then, repeat the pose on the opposite side, bringing your left knee forward and extending your right leg back.

Bridge Pose (Setu Bandhasana)

- Start by lying on your back on your yoga mat with your knees bent and feet hip-width apart.

- Keep your arms resting by your sides with your palms facing down.

- Walk your feet towards your buttocks until your heels are directly under your knees.

- Your feet should be hip-width apart and parallel to each other.

- Press firmly into your feet and engage your core muscles.

- Relax your shoulders away from your ears and lengthen your neck by gently tucking your chin towards your chest.

- On an inhalation, press into your feet and lift your hips towards the ceiling.

- Keep your knees hip-width apart and your thighs parallel to each other. Avoid letting your knees splay out to the sides.

- If it feels comfortable, you can interlace your fingers underneath your back and walk your shoulder blades closer together.

- Hold the pose for 30 seconds, or longer if it feels comfortable for you.

- Focus on maintaining a steady breath and relaxing any tension in your body.

Reclining Bound Angle Pose (Supta Baddha Konasana)

- Begin by lying on your back on a yoga mat with your knees bent and your feet flat on the floor.

- Keep your arms resting by your sides with your palms facing up.

- Exhale and allow your knees to fall out to the sides, bringing the soles of your feet together to touch.

- Allow your knees to open towards the mat, creating a diamond shape with your legs.

- Gently slide your feet closer towards your pelvis, allowing your knees to open wider towards the mat.

- You can adjust the distance between your feet and your pelvis based on your flexibility and comfort level.

- If you feel any discomfort or strain in your hips or knees, you can place yoga blocks or folded blankets underneath your thighs for support.

- Allow your arms to rest comfortably by your sides with your palms facing up.

- Close your eyes and relax your entire body, releasing any tension or tightness in your muscles.

- Hold the pose for 1 minute, or longer if it feels comfortable for you.

Twisting Chair Pose (Parivrtta Utkatasana)

- Begin by standing at the top of your mat with your feet together or hip-width apart.

- Inhale as you raise your arms overhead, palms facing each other, and bend your knees, coming into Chair Pose (Utkatasana).

- Keep your weight in your heels and your spine long.

- Exhale and shift your weight into your right foot, grounding down through your right heel and keeping your left foot light.

- As you inhale, bring your hands together in a prayer position (Anjali Mudra) at your heart center.

- Exhale and twist your torso to the right, bringing your left elbow to the outside of your right knee.

- Press your palms together firmly to help deepen the twist.

- Turn your head to gaze over your right shoulder, looking past your right elbow.

- Hold the pose for 5 breaths, or longer if it feels comfortable for you.

- To come out of the pose, inhale as you return to the center, bringing your hands back to the prayer position at your heart.

- Straighten your legs and release your arms down by your sides.

- Repeat the pose on the opposite side, twisting to the left.

Seated Forward Fold (Paschimottanasana)

- Begin by sitting on your yoga mat with your legs extended straight out in front of you.

- Sit up tall with your spine straight and your shoulders relaxed down away from your ears.

- Press your sitting bones firmly into the mat to root down and create a stable foundation.

- Flex your feet and engage your leg muscles by drawing your kneecaps up towards your thighs.

- As you inhale, reach your arms overhead, lengthening your spine and lifting your chest towards the ceiling.

- Keep your shoulders relaxed and your neck long.

- On an exhale, begin to hinge forward at your hips, leading with your chest. Keep your spine long as you fold forward, maintaining a flat back for as long as possible.

- Continue to fold forward as far as feels comfortable, reaching your hands towards your feet.

- You can hold onto your shins, ankles, or feet, depending on your flexibility.

- If you can't reach your feet, you can use a yoga strap or towel wrapped around your feet to help you reach.

- Hold the Seated Forward Fold for 30 seconds, or longer if it feels comfortable for you. Focus on relaxing into the pose and surrendering to the stretch.

Corpse Pose (Savasana)

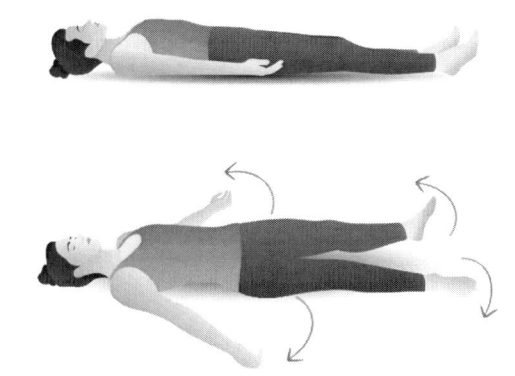

- Start by lying down on your back on your yoga mat.

- Extend your legs out straight and allow your feet to fall open naturally. Let your arms rest comfortably by your sides, palms facing up.

- Close your eyes if it feels comfortable, or soften your gaze towards the ceiling.

- Take a moment to consciously relax each part of your body, starting from your toes and working your way up to your head.

- Release any tension or tightness in your muscles, allowing your body to become heavy and completely supported by the mat.

- Adjust your body as needed to find a comfortable position in Savasana.

- You can place a bolster or rolled-up blanket under your knees for support if you have any discomfort in your lower back. You can also place a folded blanket or eye pillow over your eyes to block out any light and help you relax further.

- Bring your awareness to your breath and allow it to become slow, deep, and natural.

- Remain in Savasana for 5 minutes, or longer if time allows.

Mindfulness Practices for Cultivating Emotional Resilience

Here, we will be exploring mindfulness practices specifically designed to improve your emotional resilience, which is an important part of holistic well-being in the Somatic Yoga tradition.

One of the foundational techniques we'll get into is emotion-focused meditation. Here, you will learn to approach your emotional experiences with a stance of mindful observation rather than getting swept away by reactivity. By simply acknowledging the arising sensations and feelings without judgment or attempts to change them, you can gradually build the capacity to witness your emotions with clarity and compassion.

This practice of "emotional equanimity" has been shown to have great benefits for mental health, as mindfulness-based interventions can significantly reduce symptoms of anxiety, depression, and emotional dysregulation by enhancing one's ability to respond skillfully to challenging affective states (Keng et al., 2011).

Complementing this emotion-focused work, we have the power of gratitude practices. We can use it by consciously shifting our attention to the positive aspects of our lives. Even amid difficulties, we can rewire our neural pathways to accentuate the good and cultivate a more optimistic, resilient mindset. Its power lies in its ability to shift our focus from what's lacking or not going well to a recognition and appreciation of the good that is already present in our lives. When we're caught in the grip of stress and negative emotions, it's all too easy to get tunnel vision, fixating on our problems and overlooking the many small miracles and moments of grace that are unfolding around us all the time.

One simple yet potent way to begin incorporating gratitude into your daily routine is to keep a gratitude journal (which is a journal where you write your progress but we will talk about that later in the book). Each day, take a few minutes to reflect on and write down three to five things you're grateful for. These can be big or small, profound or mundane; the key is to really feel the sense of appreciation and wonderment they evoke within you. As you write, let yourself linger on each item, savoring the feelings of warmth, joy, and expansiveness that come to you. You might reflect on the beauty of a sunrise, the kindness of a friend, the comfort of a warm bed, or the miracle of your own beating heart. The more specific and sensory you can be in your descriptions, the more fully you'll be able to evoke a sense of gratitude in your body and mind.

Of course, practicing gratitude isn't about denying or suppressing difficult emotions, but rather learning to hold them within a larger context of appreciation and wonder. You have to open the full spectrum of our human experience with mindfulness and compassion. And with that, we develop a more balanced and resilient heart, one that can embrace both the joys and sorrows of life.

Self-Compassion Practices for Emotional Healing

This chapter's last section will look at self-compassion exercises for emotional recovery. Metta, or loving-kindness meditation, is one of the fundamental practices here. During this exercise, we recite loving-kindness sentences to ourselves initially, and then we progressively broaden the circle of compassion to encompass our loved ones, friends, and eventually all of humankind. Frequent practice of loving-kindness meditation has been shown to improve pleasant emotions, psychological health, and self-compassion. This practice helps offset the isolation and self-criticism that can lead to emotional suffering by creating a sense of unconditional acceptance and togetherness.

In addition to using love-kindness mantras on a daily basis, you may enhance their calming effects by giving yourself a nice massage. You may do this by giving your own body gentle caresses and attention. By doing so, we can trigger the parasympathetic nervous system, which facilitates relaxation, digestion, and healing. So, in times of emotional upheaval, this self-care practice might be an incredibly consoling cure (Field, 2014). Another excellent technique for developing self-compassion for emotional healing is through affirmations. Here, we intentionally swap out depressing self-talk for strong, uplifting statements, eventually changing our inner monologue and developing a more "upbeat" and self-compassionate outlook. You can rewire your ingrained habits and beliefs with these verbal and energetic techniques and promote emotional resilience and overall well-being.

Now, doing all of these practices together can really help with our emotional healing and growth. And by learning to understand and greet ourselves with kindness, acceptance, and a nurturing presence, we can actually start healing.

As we wrap up this chapter, we've seen how the mind and body are connected in a bidirectional feedback loop: our emotional experiences may be expressed physically as tensions and feelings, and our mood and emotional state can be greatly influenced by how we hold our bodies. We've looked at a variety of mindfulness-based approaches, such as emotion-focused meditation and gratitude exercises, which offer effective means of monitoring our emotions with compassion and clarity rather than letting them control us. Furthermore, practicing self-compassion via activities like self-massage and loving-kindness meditation creates self-acceptance and self-care that are crucial for emotional development and recovery. When combined, these Somatic Yoga techniques offer a thorough framework for dealing with the underlying causes of emotional imbalances. This enables us to let go of long-held tensions and blocks and, in the end, reestablish a strong sense of resilience and inner calmness.

In the following chapter, we will dive into the Somatic Yoga poses and sequences specifically designed to relieve physical stress and tension. These are body-centered techniques, and with the emotional self-regulation skills we've developed, we can continue to explore the mind-body connection.

Chapter Five

Somatic Poses for Stress and Tension Relief

Chronic stress is a problem that has become widespread in today's society. With millions of people's health and well-being at risk, this common illness has emerged as the modern plague, with women frequently suffering the most severe consequences.

The obligations that modern society places on women are too much to bear. In addition to being expected to do very well in their employment, they often endure a disproportionate amount of home obligations, balancing childcare, house duties, and providing care for elderly relatives while still making an effort to take care of themselves. Too many women are forced to deal with a "perfect storm" of chronic stress as a result of this unrelenting pressure and the enduring gender disparities that still exist in our communities and workplaces.

This physical and mental load has grave effects. The main stress hormone, elevated cortisol, may have a disastrous consequence on our bodies and be a factor in many health problems, including chronic pain, cardiovascular disease, decreased immunity, and digestive disorders (McEwen, 2017). The emotional toll is as severe since mismanaged stress causes worry, despair, and a crippling sensation of exhaustion that makes it harder to deal with day-to-day obligations.

But as you would imagine, Somatic Yoga provides an answer to this contemporary epidemic of persistent stress including Somatic Yoga practices that include stress-relieving postures, breathwork, and mindfulness-based emotional regulation exercises. The goal of these techniques is to help you restore your feeling of balance, vitality, and joy—even in the face of the most trying situations.

Understanding the Physiological Effects of Stress on the Body

In order to fully appreciate the therapeutic benefits of Somatic Yoga in managing long-term stress, we must first comprehend the psychological toll that stress has on the human body. The body's intricate biological system, known as the innate stress response, first evolved to aid in our survival from danger. Thus, our sympathetic nervous system activates in response to perceived stressors, such as pressing job deadlines or contentious disagreements with someone. This sets off the body's "fight-or-flight" response by releasing chemicals like cortisol and adrenaline. In order to prepare ourselves for the imagined threat, our muscles strain, our pulse rate rises, and our respiration quickens (Sapolsky, 2004). The issue is when this stress reaction turns into a chronic one, as it does for a great many people dealing with the unrelenting demands of modern life. Our bodies never go back to a relaxed, balanced state; instead, stress hormones go through our systems constantly, keeping us always on high alert.

Chronic muscle tension leads to debilitating headaches and back pain, while the digestive system becomes disrupted, contributing to a host of gastrointestinal issues. Furthermore, the constant strain on the cardiovascular system increases the risk of hypertension and heart disease, while the immune system's functioning is severely compromised, leaving us vulnerable to illness and infection (McEwen, 1998).

And as you know, chronic stress takes a toll on our mental health as well as emotional well-being. The prolonged exposure to elevated cortisol levels in our body has been studied several times, and most research conclusions lead to the same issue: diminished cognitive function, impaired mood regulation, and at times, leads to the development of anxiety and depression (Lupien et al., 2009).

However, Somatic Yoga can revert, or at least mitigate some of these issues through its practices and can counteract the psychological effects of stress, activating the parasympathetic nervous system and restoring the body's natural balance (Streeter et al., 2012). One other key mechanism at play is the stimulation of the parasympathetic nervous system, which governs our "rest and digest" functions. Evidence has shown that practices like deep diaphragmatic breathing, gentle stretching, and meditation can activate the vagus nerve, a major component of the parasympathetic nervous system, leading to a reduction in stress hormones like cortisol and an overall sense of relaxation and calm.

Moreover, Somatic Yoga practices that emphasize body awareness and interoception (the sense of the internal state of the body) have been shown to enhance our capacity for emotional regulation and resilience. By learning to adjust to our bodily sensations with curiosity and non-judgment, we promote a greater ability to ride the waves of challenging emotions without getting overwhelmed or reactive (Price & Hooven, 2018).

Somatic Yoga Sequences for Releasing Tension from the Neck, Shoulders, and Back

Okay, so let's look at some Somatic Yoga exercises that will help you release tension on your shoulders, neck, and back.

Seated Neck Release

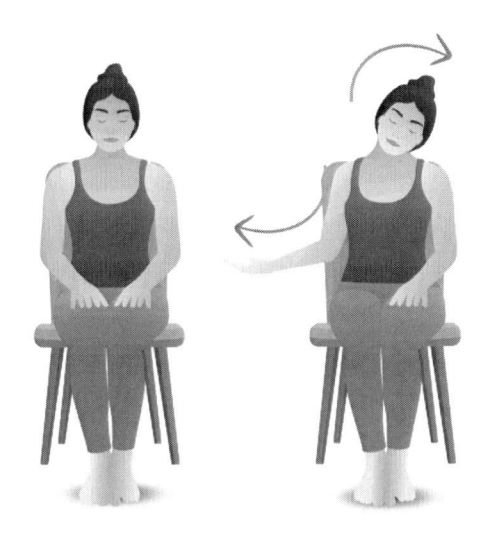

- First, sit in a comfortable position with your back straight and shoulders relaxed.

- Drop your right ear toward your right shoulder, feeling a stretch along the left side of your neck.

- Extend your left arm out to your side, palm facing up, and elbow slightly bent.

- Draw consciousness to your breath.

- Hold this position for 8 full breath counts, then switch to the other side.

Shoulder Rolls

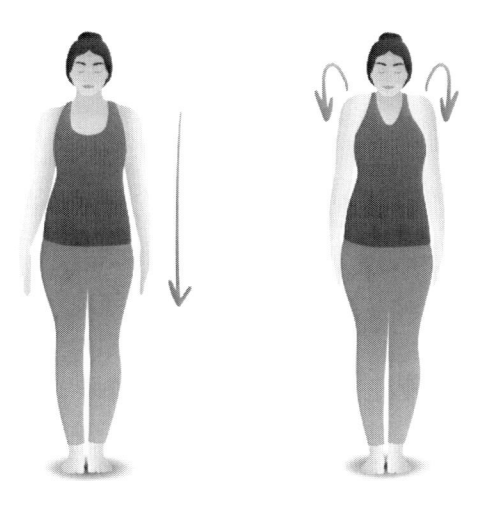

- Here, you can either sit comfortably or stand as long as your spine is straight.

- Straighten your arms in front of your thighs if standing, or knees if seated, with your palms facing away from your body.

- Inhale and lift your shoulders up toward your ears.

- Then, exhale, and roll your shoulder back and down in a smooth circular motion.

- Repeat this movement for 10 repetitions, then reverse the direction of the motion.

Thread the Needle Pose (Parsva Balasana)

- Start on your hands and knees in a tabletop position.

- As you inhale, raise your right arm up toward the ceiling, keeping both arms straight and feeling the stretch in your sides and spine.

- Turn your head and gaze up to your right hand.

- As you exhale, slide your right arm underneath your left arm, lowering your right shoulder and temple to the mat.

- Bend your left arm slightly to comfortably maintain your pose.

- As you inhale, push up with your left arm and raise your right arm toward the ceiling once more.

- Complete 5 repetitions with your right arm before switching to the other side and completing 5 repetitions with your left arm.

Extended Puppy Pose (Uttana Shishosana)

- Begin in a tabletop position with your wrists under your shoulders and knees under your hips.

- Walk your hands forward, slowly lowering your chest towards the mat while keeping your hips stacked over your knees.

- Rest your forehead or chin on the mat and extend your arms forward, feeling a stretch through your shoulders and spine.

- Slowly begin pushing your behind up toward the ceiling but keep your knees planted on the ground.

- Gently arch your back to deepen your pose.

- Hold your pose for 8 full, deep breath counts.

Supported Fish Pose

You will require a yoga block or cushion for this pose.

- Sit on the floor with your legs extended out in front of you.

- Place a yoga block or cushion behind you horizontally and in line with your mid-back.

- Slowly lower your upper back onto the support, allowing your head to rest comfortably on the floor.

- Extend your arms out to your side, palms facing up.

- Try to engage your core as you breathe deeply, filling your lungs with air.

- Lie prone in this position for 10 full breath counts.

Supine Twist (Supta Matsyendrasana)

- Lie on your back with your right knee bent, your foot flat on the floor, and your left leg straight out in front of you.

- Extend your arms out to your sides in a T-position.

- Slowly begin twisting your right knee over your left thigh, using your hips and ensuring your shoulders remain grounded.

- Use your left hand to anchor your right knee to the ground and turn your head to the right for a deeper stretch.

- Hold this position for 10 full breath counts, then return to center and switch sides.

Sphinx Pose (Salamba Bhujangasana)

- Lie on your stomach with your legs extended straight out, and your feet hip-width apart.

- Place your forearms on the mat, elbows under your shoulders.

- Press into your forearms on the mat, elbows under your shoulders.

- Press into your forearms to lift your chest off the mat, keeping your shoulders relaxed away from your ears.

- Feel the stretch in your lower back and hold the pose where it feels comfortable.

- Gaze straight ahead or slightly upward.

- Hold your pose for 8 full breath counts.

Standing Forward Fold with Clasped Hands

- Stand with your feet hip-width apart and knees slightly bent.

- Clasp your hands behind your back.

- As you inhale, hinge your body forward at your hips, bending toward the floor.

- Keep your spine long and your knees slightly bent to maintain balance.

- Allow your clasped hands to lift slightly, through your shoulders and hamstrings.

- Hold your pose for 8 breath counts and return to a neutral position slowly to avoid dizziness.

Seated Forward Fold with Side Stretch

- Sit on the floor with your legs extended in front of you.

- Inhale, lengthen, and your spine.

- Exhale and open your legs to your sides, forming a v-shape.

- Inhale once more and hinge at your hips, folding forward to your right leg first.

- If you're comfortable with it, reach both your hands down toward your right foot, gently clasping the bottom of your foot.

- Pull your chest closer to your leg to deepen your stretch.

- Hold this pose for 5 full breath counts.

- Release and return to the center, sitting upright.

- Now, repeat your movement to the left side, holding for 5 full breath counts.

Legs Up the Wall Pose (Viparita Karani)

- Sit close to a wall with your side touching it.

- Slowly lie down on your back, maintaining your contact with the wall.

- Swing your legs up onto the wall as you shift your body to form an L-shape with the all.

- Extend your arms out to your sides, palms facing up toward the ceiling.

- Engage your core, close your eyes, and bring focus to your breath.

- Hold your pose for 10 to 15 full breath counts.

- To release, slowly lower your feet down the wall and twist your body.

- Sit up slowly before returning to a standing position.

Progressive Relaxation Techniques for Reducing Overall Stress Levels

With your poses now complete, you can move on to how to alleviate the burdens of chronic stress. Progressive relaxation techniques are potent mind-body practices that can provide profound relief in even the most stressful times.

The most crucial part of this is the body scan relaxation. This is a guided meditation that systematically brings awareness to each area of the physical form, prompting the musculature to soften and release long-held tensions.

You can achieve this by tuning into the sensations from the crown of the head all the way down to the soles of the feet. This progressive unwinding of the body has a cascading effect on the entire system. As you let go of physical bracing, the mental and emotional gripping begin to untangle as well. The nervous system receives the signal that it is safe to transition from a state of high alertness into one of true rest and restoration.

To practice progressive muscle relaxation:

- Find a quiet space and lie down.

- Close your eyes and take a deep breath.

- As you exhale, draw awareness to your face, noticing any tension you have in that area.

- Lightly tense the muscles in your face 3 times, imagining the tension being released.

- Next, move on to your neck, repeating your non-judgmental awareness of any tension. Take the time to massage your neck for a few seconds.

- Now move to your shoulders, arms, hands, core, glutes, and so on, until you reach your toes.

As we bring this chapter to a close, let's reflect on the impact that chronic stress can have on our physiological well-being. We've explored how the body's innate stress response, designed to help us survive immediate threats, can become utterly dysregulated in the face of our modern-day stressors. The relentless demands we navigate on a daily basis keep our systems in a perpetual state of high alert, flooding our bodies with cortisol and adrenaline. Over time, this chronic physiological stress takes a heavy toll. Muscles remain contracted and tense, setting the stage for debilitating issues like headaches, back pain, and digestive distress. Our cardiovascular health becomes compromised, and our immune function is suppressed, leaving us vulnerable to a host of physical ailments. With all of this, the emotional and cognitive effects of elevated stress hormones contribute to mood disturbances, impaired focus, and a heightened risk of anxiety and depression.

However, you now possess a powerful set of tools to counter this stress cycle. Through the somatic yoga practices we've explored, you've learned how to systematically release built-up tension from your neck, shoulders, and back through mindful body scans. You've discovered the rejuvenating power of progressive relaxation techniques, which signal your nervous system to transition from fight-or-flight into a state of rest and restoration.

Chapter Six

Somatic Yoga for Strength and Flexibility

Too often in society, the pursuit of strength is misunderstood as a quest for bulk and brawn. But true strength extends far beyond the ability to lift heavy weights or display outward muscularity. Strength is about fortifying the very foundation of your physical form—your bones, your connective tissues, and your vital musculature. It's about building resilience in your body. And why is this so crucial? Because as you age, the natural processes of degeneration and loss of muscle mass and bone density can leave you increasingly frail and vulnerable. So, by training your strength through mindful, low-impact practices like somatic yoga, you actively counteract this decline, preserving your structural integrity and independence well into your later years.

However, strength alone is not enough to ensure you're thriving. You also need to prioritize flexibility—the balance of mobility, suppleness, and ease of movement. Without this vital counterpart, even the strongest physical form can become stiff, rigid, and prone to injury or impingement. True flexibility is about contorting yourself into strange shapes (though somatic yoga can certainly help with that)! It's about maintaining the fluid, graceful flow of energy and vitality through every cell of your body.

The Importance of Building Strength and Flexibility for Overall Well-Being

As you will see, working on your strength and flexibility is more than just aesthetics or physical prowess. Rather, it is a vital investment in your overall holistic well-being—one that pays dividends in virtually every aspect of your life.

A well-rounded fitness program needs to prioritize both strength and flexibility training. By building muscular strength and bone density through controlled, mindful movements, you lay the foundation for a resilient, injury-resistant physical form (Westcott, 2012). The benefits of strength and flexibility training include greater mobility, range of motion, and fluidity in the body, and have been shown to contribute to improved posture, reduced risk of musculoskeletal injuries, and even enhance athletic performance across a wide range of disciplines (Hough et al., 2009).

From a functional standpoint, the cooperation between strength and flexibility translates into a heightened capacity to navigate the world around you with grace and self-assurance. Simple tasks like carrying groceries, playing with children, or even getting up from a chair become effortless expressions of your physical prowess. The self-awareness and present-moment focus required to engage in these mindful practices serve to quiet the incessant mental chatter, reducing stress and anxiety levels. Meanwhile, the sense of empowerment that arises from moving with controlled strength and fluid grace bolsters our confidence and self-esteem.

Ultimately, by making space for strength and flexibility training within your self-care routines, you honor the body as the vessel through which you experience the fullness of life's adventures.

Somatic Yoga Poses to Increase Muscle Strength and Joint Flexibility

The following Somatic Yoga exercises will help you increase muscle strength and joint flexibility.

Warrior II Pose (Virabhadrasana II)

- Start the exercise in a standing position at the top of your mat.

- Place your right foot back, keeping it parallel to the back edge of your mat.

- Then, bend your left knee, aligning it over your ankle, while keeping your right leg straight and firm.

- Extend your arms out to the sides at shoulder height, palms facing down.

- Gaze over your left fingertips, keeping your shoulders relaxed away from your ears.

- Hold the pose for 8 breaths, then switch sides.

Chair Pose (Utkatasana)

- Stand straight with your feet either together or hip-width apart.

- Inhale, raise your arms overhead, palms facing each other or touching.

- Exhale, bend your knees, and lower your hips as if you're sitting back in a chair.

- Keep your chest lifted and weight in your heels, with your knees tracking over your toes.

- Hold for 8 full breath counts, engaging your core and thigh muscles.

Plank Pose (Phalakasana)

- Start in a push-up position with your hands shoulder-width apart, and wrists under your shoulders.

- Extend your legs straight back, toes tucked under, creating a straight line from head to heels.

- Engage your core muscles and keep your body in a straight line without sagging or arching your back.

- Hold the pose for 10 full breath counts, focusing on steady breathing and maintaining alignment.

Boat Pose (Navasana)

- Sit on the floor with your knees bent and feet flat on the mat.

- Lean back slightly, balancing on your sit bones.

- Slowly lift your feet off the mat, bringing your shins parallel to the floor and your knees slightly bent.

- Extend your arms straight out in front of you, parallel to the floor on either side of your thighs.

- Engage your core muscles to lift your chest and straighten your spine.

- Bring focus to your breath and hold your pose for up to 10 breath counts.

Downward-Facing Dog (Adho Mukha Svanasana)

- Begin in a tabletop position with your hands and knees on the mat, wrists under shoulders, and knees under hips.

- Tuck your toes onto the mat, lift your hips up and back, and straighten your arms and legs to form an inverted V shape.

- Press your palms into the mat, actively lengthen your spine, and engage your quadriceps to lift your behind toward the ceiling.

- Keep your heels flat on the ground if possible. If not, bend your knees slightly to accommodate the pose.

- Hold the pose focusing on deepening your breath and lengthening your spine for 15 full breath counts.

Extended Triangle Pose (Utthita Trikonasana)

- Start in a standing position with your feet about 3-4 feet apart, parallel to each other.

- Turn your right foot out 90 degrees and your left foot slightly inward.

- Extend your arms out to the sides at shoulder height.

- Reach your right arm forward as far as comfortable, then lower it down to rest on your right shin, ankle, or a block.

- Extend your left arm up towards the ceiling, stacking your shoulders.

- Gaze up at your left hand or down at your right foot, depending on your neck's comfort.

- Hold your position for 10 breath counts and then switch sides.

Side Plank Pose (Vasisthasana)

- Start in a plank pose with your wrists under your shoulders and your body in a straight line.

- Shift your weight onto your right hand and the outer edge of your right foot, stacking your left foot on top of the right.

- Twist your body in a controlled way and lift your left arm up toward the ceiling, stacking your shoulders and hips.

- Engage your core and lift your hips, creating a straight line from heels to head.

- Turn your head to the left and gaze at your left hand.

- Hold this pose for between 5 and 10 full breath counts before returning to the mat with both hands and repeating on the other side.

Low Lunge (Anjaneyasana)

- Begin in a plank position.

- When you're comfortable and ready, move your right foot forward between your hands, aligning your right knee over your right ankle.

- Lower your left knee to the mat, untuck your toes, and slide your left foot back until you feel a comfortable stretch in your left hip flexor.

- Lift your torso upright by hinging at your hips and raising your arms overhead.

- Hold this pose for 8 full breath counts before returning to a plank position and completing your pose on the other side.

Crow Pose (Bakasana)

This is an advanced pose and requires you to honor your body. If you would like to try this pose, make sure you're doing so safely with adequate support and cushioning below you.

- Begin the exercise in a squat position with your back near a wall, your feet slightly apart and your palms planted on the mat shoulder-width apart.

- Bend your elbows slightly and bring your knees to rest on the backs of your upper arms.

- Shift your weight forward into your hands, engage your core, and begin using the wall as leverage to lift your feet off the mat.

- Keep your gaze down to the floor, balancing your weight between your hands.

- Hold for five breath counts, then release back to the mat.

Supported Shoulder Pose

- Lie on your back with your knees bent and feet flat on the floor.

- If you believe you'll need support, place a cushion or yoga block under your lower back.

- Engage your core and begin to raise your legs up above you, keeping your knees straight.

- Place your hands on your outer hips, just above your behind to help support your weight.

- Keep your core engaged and focus on your breath.

- Hold your pose for up to 10 breath counts.

- When you're ready to disengage from the pose, do so with control by slowly lowering your pelvis and feet back to the mat.

Modifications and Variations for Practitioners of All Levels

I understand that the prospect of starting a strength and flexibility-focused Somatic Yoga practice can feel daunting, especially if you're new to the practice. However, one of the great aspects of this holistic approach is its emphasis on meeting you exactly where you are, without judgment or unrealistic expectations. The ancient teachings remind us that yoga is not about battling through poses or forcing the body into prescribed shapes. Instead, it's about exploring your unique form with compassion, wisdom, and skillful means. And here is where props and some variations come in.

What if you had access to any pose, no matter your current level of strength or flexibility, simply by employing the strategic use of blocks, straps, bolsters, or other supportive tools? Suddenly, that deep backbend you've been working toward or the full expression of a challenging balance becomes well within your reach. For those of you just beginning your somatic yoga journey, these props offer a gentle on-ramp, allowing you to experience the postures in a way that honors your body's needs and limitations.

At the same time, for the seasoned practitioners among us, the creative use of props presents an opportunity to deepen your practice in profound ways. You can leverage their support, and you'll be able to explore advanced binds, intricate alignments, and gravity-defying inversions that challenge your physical edges while remaining rooted to the core of the practice.

It all comes down to the subtle shifts of weight, the nuanced engagement of muscles, and the breath-guided transitions between shapes. These are the somatic details that transform our practice.

Now, these tools are not crutches or signs of weakness; they are skillful means to meet your body exactly where it is in this present moment. One of the most versatile aids in your toolkit is the simple yoga block. You can employ these sturdy rectangles, bringing the ground closer to us and allowing those with tighter hamstrings or limited spinal flexibility to access forward folds and other poses with integrity. For arm balances and inversions, blocks provide a stable base to work towards gradually over time.

The strap, too, acts as an extension of our limbs, opening up entirely new possibilities. Need more length to bind in a twist or struggle to grasp your feet in certain postures? The strap becomes your ally, allowing you to experience the full shape and energetic effects of a given asana, even for the most seasoned practitioner. And for those seeking profound relaxation and release, bolsters and blankets offer nurturing support. These allow the body to soften over cushioning props, and we reach the quiet stillness and introspection at the heart of the somatic experience.

Adaptations for Beginners

Let's start with standing poses like Warrior I and II. While the full expressions call for deep lunges and robust core engagement, beginners can work at building that foundational strength and stability by bending the front knee only as far as comfortable. The back foot can remain on the ground rather than turning the heel in, and the arms can extend forward rather than overhead.

Similarly, seated forward folds become gentle exercises of flexion rather than pursuits of perfection. By bending the knees generously, using the support of a bolster or blocks under the hamstrings—these adjustments comply with your body's current limits while still providing the benefits of spinal lengthening.

Let's now look at foundational postures like Downward Facing Dog for example. While the full version requires ample upper body strength and open hamstrings, we can make this shape accessible by bending the knees generously and walking the feet toward the hands. You'll still reap the benefits of lengthening the spine and building upper-body integration. When it comes to standing balances like Tree Pose, using the support of a wall allows you to steadily reach the equilibrium, focus, and ankle mobility required. From this stable foundation, you can then try lifting the opposite knee higher, week by week.

The main principle here is to never force or push past your current limits. The postures are shapes to explore mindfully, not idealized pictures to strive for. Each variation provides the opportunity to build awareness, control, and functional strength from the inside out.

Progressions for Advanced Practitioners

For those who have been walking the somatic yoga path for some time now, this strength and flexibility-focused section offers ample opportunities to deepen your practice and explore your "outer" edges in a mindful, sustainable way.

For instance, in standing poses like Warrior III, instead of simply kicking the leg back, bring your coherent focus to rooting down through the standing leg while actively extending the lifted heel towards the wall behind you. Engage the low abdominal muscles to integrate the frontline of the body. For balancing shapes like Eagle Pose, try taking the revolved variation by binding the arms behind the back and twisting the torso towards the lifted knee. Keep in mind that this exercise demands intense concentration and core control.

But again, remember, the depth of these practices is not measured by attaining pretzel-like contortions. The true progress lies in your ability to unite strength and flexibility, through every microcosmic movement with a completely harmonious presence.

As we get to the end of this chapter, I feel it's important to reiterate just how crucial the refinement of these poses are, particularly for women navigating the many demands and transitions of our lives. So often, women are conditioned to perceive strength as unfeminine or at odds with cultural ideals of beauty and grace. Yet the truth is, that fortifying your physical, emotional, and spiritual resilience through practices like Somatic Yoga is one of the most empowered acts of self-love you can embody.

Before we move on to our next chapter, I'd like to leave you with one final encouragement regarding these strength and flexibility-focused somatic practices. Consistency and dedication will be the keys that truly unlock their potential. While even a single session can provide immense value, I challenge you to find time in your busy routine for these Somatic Yoga poses at least three times per week. Treat it as a self-honoring ritual, a moving meditation that reaffirms your commitment to wholeness and vitality.

Whether first thing in the morning to greet the day with presence and resilience, or in the evening as a way to unwind and integrate after a long day, develop a rhythm that works with your life. You know that even a relatively brief 10–20 minute practice can shift your state.

Chapter Seven
Somatic Yoga for Weight Loss

There's more to Somatic Yoga than what I've been talking about so far and in this chapter, you will see how it can also help you with weight loss. Now, I want to be clear from the outset: shedding excess weight is not the ultimate aim or focus of Somatic Yoga. The path you're on aims far higher and toward a wholeness that extends far beyond any number on a scale.

However, it is also true that for many of us, our current physical circumstances may include carrying extra weight that feels burdensome or out of alignment. This imbalance can manifest not just physiologically but emotionally, mentally, and even spiritually.

So in addressing your overall well-being through the practice of Somatic Yoga, weight issues often arise organically. The reasons for this welcome side effect are many and include physical movement, better postures, and reduction in stress due to breath practices.

Exploring the Role of Somatic Yoga in Weight Management

At the heart of Somatic Yoga's potential for weight management is the development of an intimate mind-body connection. So often, our relationships with food, exercise, and our very physical forms become tense and disconnected—driven by unconscious habits, emotional triggers, and disembodied expectations imposed by society. Somatic yoga allows us to take a radically different path. Through the continuity of mindful movement, breath awareness, and introspection, we start to understand our bodies. And in doing so, something pivotal shifts within us. We start to perceive the cyclical nature of cravings, impulses, and ritualized patterns that may have previously derailed our best-laid plans. With this lucid self-awareness, we can respond with consciousness rather than routine reactivity.

The research backs up this phenomenon. Studies show that mind-body practices like Somatic Yoga can positively impact the neural pathways and hormonal regulators involved in appetitive behaviors and stress responses (Carrière et al., 2017). As our powers of mindfulness deepen, we simply become less susceptible to emotional overeating or self-sabotaging decisions rooted in dysregulation.

It goes beyond food or eating, too. We start to intuit what our entire being truly requires to thrive, be it proper sleep, stress management, gentle movement, or nurturing self-care. The disharmony that so often catalyzes weight imbalances begins to resolve itself spontaneously. So, developing this mind-body connection through practice allows us to go through life from a grounded, intuitive core instead of falling into patterns of deprivation or harsh self-judgment.

Another crucial piece of how Somatic Yoga can support weight management lies in its capacity to mitigate the effects of chronic stress. You see when we find ourselves in a perpetual state of physical, emotional, or psychological overwhelm, a cascade of physiological imbalances can ensue—including disrupted metabolic function and unhealthy weight fluctuations. The biological mechanisms at play here are deeply rooted in our evolutionary wiring. When the body perceives itself to be under acute threat or duress, it ramps up the production of the stress hormone cortisol. This biochemical shift served our ancestors well, providing a surge of energy to either fight or flee from predators. However, in our modern, chronically stressed society, that same cortisol response can quickly become maladaptive. Persistently elevated cortisol levels dysregulated insulin metabolism, increased abdominal fat deposition, and can even trigger emotional and neurological patterns that drive compulsive overeating (Torres & Nowson, 2007).

But Somatic Yoga can help us with this through the practices of mindful breathwork and movement that activate the parasympathetic nervous system—that branch devoted to rest, digest, and restore (Gard et al., 2014). So, as we rewire neurological pathways, our system resets homeostatic equilibrium. Finally, through intentional and adaptive physical form, we improve the body's capacity to metabolize and resettle in the face of stressors.

Somatic Yoga Poses to Boost Metabolism and Burn Calories

To accompany what we just talked about, let's look at some poses that can burn calories and boost your metabolism.

Mountain Pose (Tadasana)

- Begin this pose by standing tall with your feet hip-width apart and arms by your sides.

- Then, press down through your feet, engaging your leg muscles.

- Lengthen your spine, reaching the crown of your head towards the ceiling.

- Roll your shoulders back and down, opening your chest.

- Relax your face and breathe deeply, grounding yourself in the present moment.

- Hold your pose for up to 20 full breath counts.

Locust Pose (Salabhasana)

- Lie on your belly with your arms by your sides and palms facing up.

- Inhale, lift your chest, arms, and legs off the mat, keeping your face down.

- Engage your back muscles to lift higher, feeling a gentle stretch in your spine.

- When you're in a comfortable position, deepen your stretch, if possible, by reaching your hands toward each other and lifting your gaze straight ahead.

- Hold the pose for up to 15 full breath counts, then release back to the mat.

Extended Side Angle Pose (Utthita Parsvakonasana)

- Start in Warrior II pose with your right leg forward.

- Extend your right arm forward, then lower it down to rest on your right thigh, block, or the mat if you can.

- Straighten your left leg and reach your left arm overhead, creating a straight line from your left heel to your fingertips.

- Turn your palm facing down toward the ground and gaze up at your hand.

- Keep your chest open and focus on your breath.

- Hold the pose for up to 10 breath counts, then switch sides.

Wide-Legged Forward (Prasarita Padottanasana)

- Begin by standing at the top of your mat with your feet wide apart.

- Inhale, lengthening your spine.

- Exhale, hinge at your hips, and fold forward, bringing your hands to the mat or holding onto your ankles.

- Square your elbows, if possible, so that your legs form a triangle and your arms and shoulders form a rectangle

- Keep your spine long and the crown of the head reaching toward the ground.

- If you cannot comfortably complete this pose, feel free to use yoga blocks or bend your knees slightly.

- Hold for up to 8 full breath counts, feeling a stretch through your hamstrings and spine.

Warrior III Pose (Virabhadrasana III)

- Begin in a Mountain Pose.

- Shift your weight onto your right foot and lift your left leg behind you, parallel to the floor.

- Extend your arms forward, palms facing each other or touching.

- Engage your core and lengthen through your spine, creating a straight line from head to heel.

- Keep your hips square and gaze down toward the ground.

- Hold your pose for up to 15 breath counts, then change sides.

Dolphin Plank Pose

- Begin in a Downward Dog pose.

- Lower your elbows to the floor and rest on your forearms. You can bend your knees as you adjust to this position.

- Now, take a big step back with your right leg.

- Engage your core as you step back with your left leg.

- Keep your feet slightly apart and your body balanced.

- Gaze at the floor as you align your body straight from head to heels.

- Hold your pose for 8 full breath counts.

Firefly Pose (Tittibhasana)

This is an advanced pose that requires strength, balance, and stability. If you cannot lift your feet off the ground, that is perfectly acceptable. The goal is to try and advance as your body becomes stronger and more balanced.

- Begin the pose in a squat position with your feet slightly wider than hip-width apart and your toes pointing slightly outwards.

- Then, place your hands on the mat between your feet, shoulder-width apart.

- Shift your weight forward onto your hands and lift your hips.

- Bring your knees to the backs of your upper arms near your armpits.

- Lean forward, engage your core, and lift your feet off the ground.

- Straighten your arms and extend your legs out to the sides, finding balance in the pose.

- Hold and then gently release back to the mat.

Half Moon (Ardha Chandrasana)

- Begin this exercise in a Warrior II position with your right leg forward.

- Shift your weight onto your right foot and reach your left arm forward, parallel to the ground.

- Then, start shifting your weight onto your right hand and lift your leg off the ground.

- Stack your left hip over your right hip and open your chest towards the left side.

- Extend your left arm towards the sky, creating a straight line from your left heel to your fingertips.

- Keep your gaze towards your left hand or down at the ground for balance.

- Hold it for a few seconds and switch sides.

Revolved Triangle Pose (Parivrtta Trikonasana)

- Start in a standing forward fold with your feet hip-width apart.

- Place your right foot back, coming into a lunge position with your left foot forward.

- Plant your left hand on the mat or a block on the outside of your left foot.

- Inhale and reach your right arm up towards the sky.

- Exhale, twist your torso to the left.

- Keep your spine long and gaze up towards your left hand if it feels comfortable to you.

- Hold it for a few seconds and change sides.

Camel Pose (Ustrasana)

- Start by kneeling on the mat with your knees hip-width apart and the tops of your feet flat on the ground.

- Place your hands on your lower back with your fingers pointing down.

- Tne, inhale, lift your chest, and arch your back, pressing your hips forward.

- If comfortable, reach your hands back to grasp your heels one at a time.

- Keep your neck long and gaze up or slightly back.

- Hold for several breaths, then release by bringing your hands back to your lower back and slowly sitting back onto your heels.

Cooling Down With Somatic Stretches

Cooling down provides you with an opportunity to re-emerge from your somatic yoga practices gently and without the risk of injury. Again, these stretches can be used as a stand-alone practice or as a way to cool your body down before continuing with your day.

Up-Dog Stretch

- Begin by lying face down on the floor with your legs extended behind you and the tops of your feet resting on the ground.

- Place your hands on the floor beside your ribs, fingers spread wide and pointing forward, with your elbows close to your body.

- Inhale deeply, then exhale as you press into your hands and straighten your arms, lifting your chest and upper body off the floor.

- Keep your shoulders relaxed and away from your ears, allowing your chest to open and your shoulder blades to draw together.

- Straighten your arms fully, but be sure to avoid locking your elbows.

- Press the tops of your feet into the floor to lift your thighs off the ground, engaging your leg muscles.

- Keep your gaze forward or slightly upward, avoiding straining your neck.

- Hold the up-dog position for up to 15 breath counts.

- To release, exhale as you slowly lower your chest back down to the floor, returning to the starting position.

- Rest in a neutral position for a moment before repeating the stretch or moving into another pose.

Spinal Roll Stretch

- Begin by lying on the floor with your legs extended in front of you and your spine tall.

- Bend your knees and lift your body off the floor, grabbing on to your knees and lifting your feet off the floor.

- Inhale deeply, then exhale as you slowly begin to round your spine, starting from your tailbone and moving sequentially through each vertebra.

- Allow your chin to drop slightly toward your chest as you continue to round forward, bringing your torso towards your thighs.

- Hold the rounded position for a moment, feeling a stretch along your spine and the back of your body.

- Inhale again, then exhale as you reverse the movement, slowly unrolling your spine one vertebra at a time.

- Repeat the spinal roll for 2-3 more repetitions, moving with your breath and paying attention to any areas of tension or tightness.

Armpit Stretch

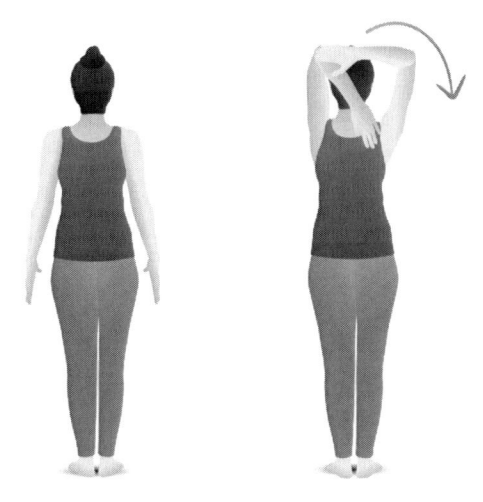

- Start by standing tall with your feet hip-width apart and your arms by your sides.

- Lift your right arm overhead, bending it at the elbow so that your hand reaches toward your upper back.

- Bend your left arm and reach behind your back, aiming to grasp your right elbow or forearm with your left hand.

- Gently pull your right elbow towards your head, feeling a stretch along the underside of your right arm and into your armpit.

- Keep your shoulders relaxed and your chest open as you hold the stretch for up to 10 breath counts.

- Release the stretch and switch sides, lifting your left arm overhead and reaching behind your back with your right hand to grasp your left elbow or forearm.

Chest Stretch

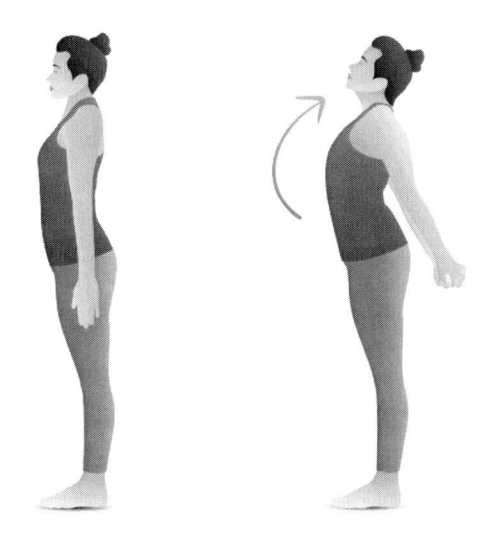

- Begin by standing tall with your feet hip-width apart and your shoulders relaxed.

- Reach both arms behind your back and clasp your hands together, interlacing your fingers.

- Straighten your arms as much as possible, gently pulling your hands away from your body.

- Keep your chest open and your shoulders down away from your ears.

- As you press your hands away from your body, you should feel a stretch across the front of your chest and shoulders.

- Hold the stretch for 10 breath counts.

- Avoid arching your lower back or leaning forward; instead, keep your spine tall and your core engaged.

- If you're unable to clasp your hands together, you can use a towel or yoga strap to bridge the gap between your hands.

- Release the stretch and gently shake out your arms before repeating as needed.

Butterfly Stretch

- Sit on the floor with your knees bent and the soles of your feet together, allowing your knees to fall open to the sides.

- Hold onto your ankles or feet with your hands, depending on your flexibility.

- Sit up tall, lengthening your spine, and engage your core muscles to support your lower back.

- Gently press your knees towards the floor using your elbows, but avoid forcing them down.

- Feel a stretch through your inner thighs and groin area.

- Keep your chest lifted and your shoulders relaxed away from your ears.

- Hold the stretch for up to 30 breath counts.

- If you want to deepen the stretch, you can gently lean your torso forward, keeping your back straight.

- However, be mindful not to round your spine excessively or strain your neck.

- Relax into the stretch, allowing your muscles to release tension.

- Slowly sit back up and release the stretch, shaking out your legs if needed.

Mindful Eating Practices to Support Sustainable Weight Loss

To be able to fully realize what Somatic Yoga has to offer, we need to work on our mindset and this means understanding the intuitive relationship between food and our appetite. For too long, we've been conditioned to view eating as an indulgence requiring discipline and restriction. But not anymore and instead we can engage in nourishment from a place of presence, wisdom, and listening to our body's innate intelligence.

One of the main principles we'll explore in this section is intuitive eating—the radical act of understanding the cues of hunger, satiety, and what our being truly needs in any given moment instead of adhering to rigid diets or extrinsic rules. Those who adopt an intuitive eating approach tend to have lower BMIs, higher HDL cholesterol levels, and an overall more positive body image compared to those trapped in cycles of restrictive eating (Bruce & Ricciardelli, 2016). By relearning to trust our inner guide, we transcend the need for deprivation or struggle around food.

To complement this intuitive eating, we need to get into mindful consumption techniques centered on slowing down and savoring each delectable bite. Instead of shoveling fuel in a dissociated daze, we bring full sensory awareness to the flavors, textures, temperatures, and even the sounds of mastication. This simple act of presence not only enhances our enjoyment but also triggers the hormones that signal satiety and satisfaction. With this, we can develop somatic awareness around our responses to hunger pains, food cravings, feelings of fullness, or discomfort—this is where we begin to reprogram the unconscious patterns and habits that may have sabotaged our efforts in the past. With practice, this recalibration ripples out to enhance our relationships with exercise, stress management, sleep, and every other area that impacts our weight and overall well-being.

Portion Control and Mindful Snacking

Building upon the foundations of intuitive eating and conscious consumption above, let's now explore some practical mindful eating tools to support sustainable, holistic weight attunement.

When it comes to portion control, the somatic approach isn't about rigid restriction or deprivation. Instead, we should focus on appropriate serving sizes and learn to respect our body's natural signals of hunger and fullness. One powerful method is to use smaller plates and bowls. Numerous studies have shown that people unconsciously consume more food when served on larger dishes (Hollands et al., 2015). So, by downsizing our plates, we can avoid overeating simply from visual illusion.

Getting familiar with things like measuring out grain and protein servings and what a cupped handful looks like for denser items like nuts and seeds is part of the process. The same is true for snacking—an area that can so easily derail our efforts if not approached with consciousness.

For instance, nourishing snack ideas that can help you satisfy true hunger while providing a bounty of vitamins, minerals, fiber, and healthy fats are a great start. Fresh fruits like apples, berries, or citrus make for sweet treats loaded with antioxidants. Other snacks, such as lightly salted nuts and seeds that offer satiating protein and good fats, or even some crunchy veggie sticks like carrots, cucumbers, or jicama, can hit that savory, crispy craving.

Having these whole food options prepared and easily accessible is half the battle. That way, when biological hunger strikes between meals, you can avoid turning to highly processed, refined snacks that only lead to continued cravings and potential overeating. But beyond just swapping chips for carrot sticks, developing your snacking tendencies is just as important. Before automatically reaching for that bag or box of snacks, you should pause to tune into the signals your body is sending.

Is this a deep, grumbling belly hunger that's building slowly? Or is it more of a restless, urgent craving stemming from stress, boredom, or emotional discomfort? Getting good at making this distinction is huge. If it's true nutritional hunger, then by all means, choose one of those prepared whole food snacks we discussed and bring your full mindful presence to consuming it. Savor each bite, texture, and flavor without distraction or guilt.

However, if we detect that the urge to snack is more for self-soothing or avoidance, that's our cue to get radically curious and try to understand what's arising inside. Is there an unmet need demanding our attention? An emotion that we've been trying to numb out or push away? By simply inquiring, we can then apply any number of Somatic Yoga tools—maybe it's breathwork, movement, journaling, or positive self-talk. Basically, anything that allows us to ride that urge mindfully rather than compulsively acting on it. In doing so, we reprogram those unconscious, self-sabotaging patterns that keep us stuck.

Before we move on to the next chapter, I want to restate one of the main truths we've looked at here—that going down this path is not about deprivation, struggle, or putting yourself at war with your own being. Instead, with the exercises and the tips I gave you, you should approach the subjects of weight and nutrition with a calmer demeanor and understand what your body needs instead of just indulging in disproportionate eating.

We've also seen how understanding the mind-body connection counteracts the unconscious cravings, emotional triggers, and self-sabotaging patterns that often derail our efforts. As you realize the present moment, you gain the ability to respond to hunger, stress, and life's challenges with more knowledge. The mindful eating practices of intuitive consumption, conscious portioning, and defusing emotional snacking provide a toolkit for rekindling an intuitive, trusting relationship with food and our appetites. No more battling ourselves through deprivation—only the natural unfolding of our being's innate, bodily intelligence.

Of course, we also looked at how intentional somatic shapes, breathwork, and self-inquiry can equip us to transform the chronic stressors and psycho-emotional roots that so often facilitate weight imbalances in the first place. So if sustainable, the practice does emerge as a side-effect of walking this path—whether that means effortless, gradual inch loss or simply experiencing your current form with greater ease—it will arise not through battling or self-inflicted suffering, but through nourishment, self-care, and honoring the truth of who you are.

In our next chapter, we'll explore how to solidify all these teachings into an immersive 21-day somatic evolution protocol.

Chapter Eight

Your 21-Day Somatic Evolution

In this chapter, we will be looking at an immersive 21-day somatic plan designed to solidify everything we've learned so far including how you can better integrate the holistic somatic experience to habit-forming daily practices. As human beings, we are profoundly influenced by the habits and routines we create in our lives. Our brains naturally encode the behavioral patterns we repeat most frequently, allowing us to conduct certain actions with minimal conscious effort. This frees up our mental bandwidth for other pursuits.

However, this same neurological hard-wiring can just as easily entrench habits and patterns that do not serve our greatest well-being and growth. That's why undertaking a structured, purposeful plan for a concentrated period of time can be so catalytic. By committing to a routine of daily Somatic Yoga practices over the course of 21 consecutive days, we create the foundations for new neural pathways to be forged. Those empowering thoughts, movements, and mindfulness techniques get encoded as our new "normal" through repetition.

There's something particularly powerful about that three-week timeframe. It's widely considered the bare minimum period for a new behavior to settle in and start becoming automated into our neurocircuitry and sticking with us over the long term (Lally et al., 2010). So think of these upcoming 21 days as an initiation—like a ceremonial shedding of old patterns and a rebirth into higher levels of wisdom, vitality, and self-actualization. Each day will build upon the next until the practices become automated. After that, you'll awaken to new degrees of somatic awareness and presence. You'll experience insights and breakthroughs that have been waiting to unveil themselves. And perhaps most importantly, you'll forge habits that become not just part of your routine but part of your identity.

So prepare your mind, body, and spirit to embark upon this 21-day somatic evolution. All the teachings have prepared you for this great unfolding. Now it's time to surrender to it.

As we begin this 21-day somatic evolution, I want to remind you that what lies ahead is nothing less than your own personal revolution. A metamorphosis so transformative that life as you've known it will never be the same. For far too long, you've been held captive by unconscious patterns, self-limiting beliefs, and contractions that have kept you from thriving in your life. But now, you are reclaiming your birthright as a sacred, sovereign being through these somatic practices.

Over the course of these 21 days, you will quite literally re-wire your neurocircuitry, re-sculpt your musculature, and re-encode your being through sustained, conscious practice. Each intentional breath, each mindful movement, and each act of self-inquiry will forge new neural pathways of unshakable presence and aliveness. This is not merely another wellness program or self-help regimen. No, what you are undertaking here is an initiatory odyssey. A heroine's journey into the depths of your being, armed with the tools of Somatic Yoga as your ally.

Each step along this path will reveal challenges to be overcome and rewards to be realized. Your emotional landscape will be achieved through practices of mindful awareness and self-compassion. And your existential identity will evolve into self-sovereignty.

Free Somatic Workbook

As a special gift for our readers, I'm offering a complimentary Somatic Workbook to increase your understanding and practice of the concepts presented in this book. The workbook is designed to guide you through a series of exercises and reflections that will help you develop a deeper connection with your body and mind.
To access your free Somatic Workbook, simply scan the QR code below using your smartphone's camera or QR code reader app. You will be directed to a private webpage where you can download the workbook.

Overview of the Structure

Let me first give you an overview of the structure that will guide our 21-day somatic evolution path. Think of this as a map to understand what you will go through during the next three weeks.

The first 7 days, collectively known as the "Foundations of Somatic Yoga Practice" week, will start you into the core practices that shall become your daily anchors. Each morning, you'll be guided through an intention-setting practice to align your energy with the theme for that day. This somatic "coding" lays the metaphysical runway for your transformation to unfold. Here, we will also explore breathwork techniques like Nadi Shodhana, Kapalabhati, and other pranayama practices. These breath-based exercises activate your energies and begin restructuring your consciousness.

Having anchored the foundational elements, this cycle intensifies the frequencies. The first three days of the second week are centered on "Building Strength and Flexibility" through invigorating vinyasa flow sequences, core cultivation, and mobility work. Fortifying your physical form becomes the goal. The following four days focus squarely on working on your emotional resilience and practices like loving-kindness meditation.

In this final phase, the path turns inward for deep somatic embodiment. The first part of the third week is centered on integrating mindfulness into your daily life with activities like yoga nidra, journaling, and establishing nurturing routines. The remainder of our journey revolves around reflecting on the journey you've undertaken. Restorative practices, artistic self-expression, and extended silent sits become the womb incubating your new unified identity.

SOMATIC YOGA FOR BEGINNERS

DAY	FOCUS	POSES
1	Forward Fold	Forward Fold (Uttanasana), Seated Forward Fold (Paschimottanasana), Standing Forward Fold with Clasped Hands, Wide-Legged Forward Fold (Prasarita Padottanasana), Child's Pose (Balasana)
2	Heart Opening	Heart-Opening Poses, Bridge Pose (Setu Bandhasana), Sphinx Pose (Salamba Bhujangasana), Supported Fish Pose, Camel Pose (Ustrasana)
3	Rest Day	
4	Twists and Turns	Twisting Chair Pose (Parivrtta Utkatasana), Seated Neck Release, Thread the Needle Pose (Parsva Balasana), Supine Twist (Supta Matsyendrasana), Reclining Bound Angle Pose (Supta Baddha Konasana)
5	Strength and Stability	Plank Pose (Phalakasana), Side Plank Pose (Vasisthasana), Dolphin Plank Pose, Low Lunge (Anjaneyasana), Warrior II Pose (Virabhadrasana II)
6	Balance and Focus	Warrior III Pose (Virabhadrasana III), Half Moon Pose (Ardha Chandrasana), Extended Triangle Pose (Utthita Trikonasana), Boat Pose (Navasana), Mountain Pose (Tadasana)
7	Relaxation and Meditation	Corpse Pose (Savasana), Seated Forward Fold with Side Stretch, Supported Shoulder Pose, Seated Neck Release, Shoulder Rolls
8	Leg Stretch	Downward-Facing Dog (Adho Mukha Svanasana), Legs Up the Wall Pose (Viparita Karani), Extended Puppy Pose (Uttana Shishosana), Revolved Triangle Pose (Parivrtta Trikonasana), Extended Side Angle Pose (Utthita Parsvakonasana)
9	Flow and Fluidity	Cat-Cow Pose (Marjaryasana-Bitilasana), Pigeon Pose (Eka Pada Rajakapotasana), Dolphin Plank Pose, Firefly Pose (Tittibhasana), Revolved Triangle Pose (Parivrtta Trikonasana)
10	Rest Day	

DAY	FOCUS	POSES
11	Core Strength	Boat Pose (Navasana), Plank Pose (Phalakasana), Dolphin Plank Pose, Locust Pose (Salabhasana), Crow Pose (Bakasana)
12	Stretch and Release	Forward Fold (Uttanasana), Child's Pose (Balasana), Wide-Legged Forward Fold (Prasarita Padottanasana), Seated Forward Fold (Paschimottanasana), Supine Twist (Supta Matsyendrasana)
13	Balance and Focus	Warrior III Pose (Virabhadrasana III), Half Moon Pose (Ardha Chandrasana), Extended Triangle Pose (Utthita Trikonasana), Mountain Pose (Tadasana), Downward-Facing Dog (Adho Mukha Svanasana)
14	Relaxation and Meditation	Corpse Pose (Savasana), Seated Forward Fold with Side Stretch, Supported Shoulder Pose, Seated Neck Release, Shoulder Rolls
15	Forward Fold	Forward Fold (Uttanasana), Seated Forward Fold (Paschimottanasana), Standing Forward Fold with Clasped Hands, Wide-Legged Forward Fold (Prasarita Padottanasana), Child's Pose (Balasana)
16	Heart Opening	Heart-Opening Poses, Bridge Pose (Setu Bandhasana), Sphinx Pose (Salamba Bhujangasana), Supported Fish Pose, Camel Pose (Ustrasana)
17	Rest Day	
18	Twists and Turns	Twisting Chair Pose (Parivrtta Utkatasana), Seated Neck Release, Thread the Needle Pose (Parsva Balasana), Supine Twist (Supta Matsyendrasana), Reclining Bound Angle Pose (Supta Baddha Konasana)
19	Strength and Stability	Warrior III Pose (Virabhadrasana III), Half Moon Pose (Ardha Chandrasana), Extended Triangle Pose (Utthita Trikonasana), Boat Pose (Navasana), Mountain Pose (Tadasana)
20	Balance and Focus	Warrior III Pose (Virabhadrasana III), Half Moon Pose (Ardha Chandrasana), Extended Triangle Pose (Utthita Trikonasana), Boat Pose (Navasana), Mountain Pose (Tadasana)
21	Relaxation and Meditation	Corpse Pose (Savasana), Seated Forward Fold with Side Stretch, Supported Shoulder Pose, Seated Neck Release, Shoulder Rolls

Tracking Progress and Reflecting on the Journey

As you go through your 21-day somatic evolution, one of the most important tools for enhancing your journey is the practice of tracking your progress and regularly reflecting on your experiences. Here, you should bring attention to your daily practices and the turns that occur within you. So you deepen your self-awareness and retain more knowledge. A key element of this process is keeping a daily practice log. This is a sacred space where you record the details of your Somatic Yoga practices, breathwork exercises, and mindfulness activities each day. You might note the specific postures or sequences you explored, the length of your practice, and any particular focus or intention you held.

Now, beyond just the logistical details, your practice log is an opportunity to capture your subjective experiences and observations. You can reflect on how your body feels in different postures, writing down areas of ease or resistance. You can describe the quality of your breathing and any emotions or sensations that arose during your breathwork. You can also record insights or challenges that emerged during your practices. Over time, your practice log becomes a valuable map of your somatic evolution journey. But you need to review your entries. And only then, do you start to notice patterns and progressions in your experience. You might observe how your flexibility and strength gradually increase, or how your capacity for emotional regulation and mindful presence deepens.

This awareness allows you to understand your growth and achievements, as well as reinforce your commitment to the path. It also helps you identify areas where you may need to focus more, allowing you to adjust your practice. In addition to your daily log, taking time for regular reflective check-ins is also highly beneficial. On a weekly basis, you might review your log entries and spend some time in contemplative writing or meditation, exploring the overarching themes and insights that are emerging.

You can ask yourself questions like What has been the most challenging aspect of my practice this week? Where have I noticed the greatest sense of opening or release? What am I learning about myself and my habitual patterns? How is my somatic practice influencing my daily life and relationships? By engaging in this reflective process, you get a deeper understanding of your own unique journey. You start to recognize the ways in which your somatic evolution is unfolding, both on and off the mat. You also develop a more intimate relationship with yourself, learning to listen to your body's wisdom and respond accordingly.

As you move through your 21-day journey, let your practice log and reflective check-ins be your companions. Honor the process of tracking and reflecting as an essential part of your transformative path. Trust that by bringing mindful awareness to your experience, you are planting the seeds for profound growth and awakening.

Let's break the reflections into weeks. These are just examples of what you should be asking yourself throughout the different weeks of your 21-day journey, you are welcome to change them as you see fit.

Week 1 Reflections

- What has been the most surprising aspect of my Somatic Yoga practice this week?
- Where in my body do I feel the most sense of opening or release?
- What patterns of thought or emotion have I become aware of during my practice?
- How is my breath influencing my state of mind and energy levels?
- What insights are emerging about my relationship with my body and myself?

Week 2 Reflections

- What challenges have arisen in my practice this week, and how have I navigated them?
- Where am I noticing increased strength and flexibility, both physically and mentally?
- What emotions or memories have surfaced during my practice, and how have I held space for them?
- How is my somatic practice influencing my sense of self-compassion and resilience?
- What new perspectives or understandings are dawning about my habitual ways

of being?

Week 3 Reflections

- What have been the most transformative moments or breakthroughs in my journey so far?

- How has my relationship with my body and breath shifted over the course of this journey?

- What insights have I gained about my capacity for presence and mindful awareness?

- In what ways am I bringing the lessons of my somatic practice into my daily life and interactions?

- What intentions or visions are emerging for how I want to continue my somatic evolution beyond this 21-day journey?

As you engage with these reflective questions, let yourself write freely and without judgment. Trust that whatever arises is exactly what needs to be seen and acknowledged in that moment. You might find it helpful to set aside a specific time each week for this reflective practice, creating a space of quietude. Remember, the goal of reflection is not to analyze or critique your experience but rather to grow a deep listening presence.

Through these three weeks, it's essential to pause and celebrate the milestones and achievements that mark your path. You can do this by taking time to acknowledge your progress, reinforce your commitment to growth, and inspire yourself to continue embracing the transformative process.

Throughout your journey, there will be numerous opportunities to celebrate your success. These milestones might include. But are certainly not limited to:

- Completing your daily practice for a full week without missing a day

- Noticing an increase in your physical strength, flexibility, or stamina

- Experiencing a breakthrough in your emotional or mental resilience

- Having a moment of profound insight or spiritual connection during your practice

- Successfully integrating a new mindfulness habit into your daily routine
- Reaching the halfway point of your 21-day journey
- Completing the full 21-day evolution with dedication and presence

Each of these milestones, no matter how small they may seem, is a testament to your commitment and courage. They represent the steps you are taking toward greater self-awareness and wholeness. And by pausing to celebrate them, you establish the positive shifts that are occurring and fuel your motivation to keep going.

So how can you celebrate these milestones in a meaningful way? Here are a few ideas:

- Take a moment after your practice to close your eyes, place a hand on your heart, and offer yourself a silent word of appreciation or congratulations.
- Write a note of gratitude to yourself in your practice journal, acknowledging your efforts and achievements.
- Share your milestone with a supportive friend or loved one, inviting them to celebrate with you.
- Treat yourself to a nourishing act of self-care, like a warm bath, a favorite healthy meal, or a gentle massage.
- Create a simple ritual to mark the milestone, like lighting a candle, saying a prayer, or setting a new intention.
- Give yourself a day of rest or a lighter practice to integrate and savor the progress you've made.

Remember, the way you choose to celebrate is less important than the act of celebrating itself. Just by taking time to honor your journey, you are affirming to yourself that your growth and well-being are worthy of recognition and joy. As you move through your 21-day evolution, let celebration be a regular part of your practice. Allow yourself to feel the satisfaction and pride that come from showing up for yourself with dedication and love. Trust that each milestone, however small, is a reflection of the change that is unfolding within you. And as you celebrate, remember to extend that same appreciation and gratitude to your body, your breathing, and the wisdom of your somatic experience. Honor the journey itself, with all its challenges and triumphs, knowing that it is shaping you into an ever-more authentic expression of your deepest self.

As we come to the close of this 21-day somatic evolution chapter, I want to acknowledge the courage and commitment you've shown in taking on this adventure. Whether you've gone through it, are going through it, or will in the future, you have to listen to and meet yourself with compassion and curiosity. You have strengthened your body, calmed your mind, and opened your heart, and with that, you've planted the seed for more change. And yet, as impactful as these three weeks have been (or will be), this is just the beginning. The true change comes from your choice to integrate and sustain the practices and insights you've gained in your daily life moving forward.

The path of somatic awakening is not a destination to be reached but a lifelong journey of ever-deepening presence and self-discovery. It's a continuous path to show up for yourself with loving attention, to meet each moment with fresh eyes and an open heart, and to let the knowledge of yourself guide you toward greater wholeness and well-being. So as you step forward from this 21-day container, I encourage you to keep the flame of your practice alive. Continue to carve out time each day, even if just for a few mindful breaths or gentle movements, to reconnect with your body and your inner landscape. Keep exploring the practices that resonate most deeply with you, whether it's a particular yoga sequence, a breathwork technique, or a mindfulness exercise.

Let the lessons you've learned during these 21 days integrate into your daily life, your relationships, and your sense of purpose. Notice how your increased somatic awareness and self-compassion ripple out into all areas of your being, creating more harmony, vitality, and joy. And trust that as you continue to show up for your practice with dedication and love, it will continue to deepen and evolve, revealing new layers of insight and transformation.

In the next and last chapter, we will talk about your future with Somatic Yoga and how you can continue to incorporate other goals to keep yourself motivated.

Chapter Nine

Your Future Using Somatic Yoga

Having completed your 21-day evolution, you now stand in a powerful position—a place where the seeds you've planted can blossom into a lifelong practice of awakening and change.

As we step into this visioning space, I invite you to reflect on the shifts and insights you've experienced over the past three weeks. Consider how things have evolved. Notice the new depths of presence, resilience, and self-understanding you've acquired. So as we look to the future of your Somatic Yoga journey, it's essential to bring a sense of intention and vision to the path ahead. To do this, you have to set clear, heartfelt goals for your ongoing practice. You create a north star that keeps you following the right path toward your deepest aspirations for growth.

These goals can be as simple or as expansive as feels authentic to you. Perhaps you want to commit to a daily practice of mindful movement and breathwork or explore new depths of emotional and spiritual healing through your somatic exercises. Or maybe you envision sharing the gifts of this practice with others or integrating its principles into your work and relationships. Whatever your unique vision may be, the key is to let it come to you from a place of truth. Listen deeply to yourself, and to let your goals be a reflection of your values and desires.

As you consider your future path, I encourage you to approach the process with a sense of curiosity, openness, and self-compassion. Remember that setting goals is not about striving for perfection or imposing rigid expectations on yourself. It's about creating a framework for your ongoing evolution. Trust that your somatic practice itself will be your greatest guide and ally in this visioning process. As you continue to show up on the mat with presence and devotion, your inner clarity and sense of purpose will naturally deepen and unfold. So take some time in the days and weeks ahead to sit with your aspirations, journal about your hopes and dreams, and let your future path reveal itself with gentleness and grace. Know that every small step you take, every moment of mindful awareness and care, is a profound act of self-love and service to the world.

As we move forward in this chapter, we'll explore some practical tools and strategies for bringing your goals to life and sustaining your practice over time. But for now, simply let yourself rest in the spaciousness of possibility, trusting that your journey will continue to unfold in perfect rhythm and timing.

However, before that, let's discuss how you can incorporate other forms of movement and mindful practices to help establish your health and well-being in the future. For instance, perhaps you feel called to explore the flowing grace of tai chi or the dynamic power of qigong, ancient Chinese practices that help inner balance, strength, and vitality. Or maybe your body yearns for the freedom and expression of dance, allowing you to move with joy and creativity. You might also feel drawn to the centering presence of walking meditation, the primal release of ecstatic movement, or the gentle rejuvenation of restorative yoga. The key is to listen to your body and to follow the forms of movement that truly resonate with you.

Beyond the physical practice, there are countless other tools and techniques that can support your ongoing growth and well-being. From journaling and creative self-expression, as I've mentioned before, to spending time in nature and connecting with loved ones, each act of mindful living is an opportunity to deepen your relationship with yourself and the world around you. You may find that your Somatic Yoga practice naturally inspires you to make other positive changes in your life, such as adopting a more nourishing diet, creating a regular sleep routine, or creating a daily gratitude practice. Trust that as you continue to show up for yourself with presence, your path will unravel in perfect alignment with your deepest values and needs.

The most important thing is to stay connected to your own inner guidance system, to listen closely to your body and mind, and to let your intuition be your compass.

Setting Intentions for Long-Term Mind-Body Wellness

As you look at your future somatic yoga journey, one of the most powerful steps you can take is to clarify your intentions for long-term mind-body wellness. You have to take time to reflect on your goals and aspirations, and with that, you create a solid foundation for your ongoing practice.

To begin this process, find a quiet space where you can sit comfortably and turn your attention inward. Take a few deep breaths, allowing your body to settle and your mind to grow still. Then, ask yourself the following questions, being sure to listen closely to the wisdom that arises from within:

- What does optimal mind-body wellness look and feel like for me?
- What are the qualities of physical, emotional, and mental well-being that I most long to cultivate in my life?
- How do I want to feel in my body on a daily basis—energized, flexible, strong, calm, or something entirely different?
- What are the aspects of my current state of health and well-being that I would like to shift or transform?
- What are the deeper values and life aspirations that my mind-body wellness practices can support me in fulfilling?

As you sit with these questions, let the answers flow freely without judgment or restriction. You might find it helpful to use your journal and write about your reflections, such as any insights, images, or feelings that arise. Remember, there are no right or wrong responses here—only the authentic stirrings of your own heart and soul. You may find that your goals for mind-body wellness are focused on specific physical outcomes, such as increased flexibility, strength, or stamina. Perhaps you long to release chronic tension or pain or to grow a greater sense of ease and freedom in your body.

Of course, physical outcomes might not be your thing at all and your aspirations might be more centered around emotional and mental well-being, such as reducing stress and anxiety, and finding greater balance and resilience in the face of life's challenges. Whatever your unique goals may be, the key is to let them align with your true self, rather than getting caught up in external metrics or expectations. Focus on the deeper qualities of being that you wish to embody—the inner states of peace, wholeness, and aliveness that are your birthright.

As you clarify your intentions for long-term mind-body wellness, I encourage you to hold them gently, with a sense of openness and flexibility. Remember that your goals are not fixed destinations to be reached but rather ever-evolving expressions of your values and desires. So take some time to sit with your reflections and connect with your deepest hopes and dreams for your mind-body wellness.

Creating a Somatic Wellness Plan

Now that you've taken time to reflect on your deepest intentions for long-term mind-body wellness, the next step is to translate those aspirations into a concrete action plan. You can craft a personalized somatic wellness plan and give yourself a clear roadmap for bringing your goals to life—a good structure that will support you in integrating your practice into your daily existence.

To begin developing your plan, consider the following key elements:

1. Daily Somatic Yoga Practice: The key to your wellness plan will be your ongoing commitment to Somatic Yoga. Reflect on what a sustainable daily practice might look like for you, taking into account your current schedule, energy levels, and life circumstances. Perhaps you dedicate 20–30 minutes each morning to mindful movement and breathwork, or you set aside time in the evening for a longer, more immersive practice. The main focus is to create a consistent rhythm that feels nourishing and achievable, one that allows you to show up for yourself with presence and devotion each day.

2. Complementary Mindfulness Practices: In addition to your somatic yoga, consider incorporating other mindfulness practices that support your overall well-being. This might include seated meditation, journaling, gratitude exercises, or spending time in nature. Again, focus on creating a realistic schedule that allows you to engage with these practices in a way that feels sustainable and enriching.

3. Self-Care Activities: A holistic wellness plan also includes regular acts of self-care. Reflect on the activities that truly fill your cup and support your physical, emotional, and mental well-being. This might include things like getting enough sleep, eating nourishing foods, spending quality time with loved ones, engaging in creative pursuits, or scheduling regular massage or bodywork sessions. Essentially, anything we've talked about before. Identify the self-care priorities that are most essential for you, and make sure to find

dedicated space for them in your plan.

4. Support Systems: Finally, consider the people, resources, and environments that will support you in bringing your wellness plan to life. This might include joining a Somatic Yoga community, working with a skilled teacher or therapist, or surrounding yourself with loved ones who share your commitment to mind-body well-being. Here, you have to identify the key pillars of support that will help you stay accountable and inspire you on your journey.

As you go through these various elements together and change them into a cohesive plan, remember to approach the process with a sense of flexibility and self-compassion. Your somatic wellness plan is meant to be a living, breathing document, one that can evolve and adapt as your needs and circumstances change. Trust that your own inner wisdom will guide you in refining your plan over time and that the practice itself will reveal new insights and possibilities along the way.

Once you have a draft of your plan, I encourage you to create a consistent exercise around setting it in motion. You might light a candle, say a prayer, or offer a symbolic gesture of commitment to your own well-being. Let this moment be a powerful affirmation of your dedication to living in greater alignment with your deepest values.

Embracing the Journey of Self-Discovery and Growth

As you continue this new phase of your Somatic Yoga journey, it's important to remember that the path you're following is not a linear progression towards a fixed goal but rather an ongoing process of self-discovery and growth. It's a journey that allows you to embrace the fullness of your human experience, with all its joys, challenges, and opportunities. So, learning to meet yourself with kindness, patience, and understanding is perhaps the greatest gift you can offer yourself as you continue to explore. Here, self-compassion means recognizing that growth takes time and that there will inevitably be moments of difficulty, resistance, and even setbacks along the way. It means letting go of the need for perfection or immediate results and instead trusting in yourself and the process.

When you approach your Somatic Yoga practice this way, you create a safe space for authentic change to happen, instead of pushing yourself to meet some external standard or expectation. This might look like giving yourself permission to rest when you're feeling depleted or modifying a challenging pose to suit your current capabilities. It might mean meeting moments of emotional intensity or mental resistance with a soft and curious gaze rather than harsh self-judgment or criticism. All of this is fine and part of the somatic way.

As you continue to nourish this quality of self-compassion on the mat, you'll likely find that it starts to permeate other areas of your life as well. You may notice that you're able to go through challenges and uncertainties with greater ease and resilience, or that you're more able to extend kindness and understanding to others in your life. However, embracing self-compassion is not always easy, especially in a world that often prioritizes self-criticism and judgment. It takes practice, patience, and a willingness to soften into the vulnerable places within ourselves. But as you continue to show up for yourself, you'll find that self-compassion becomes an increasingly natural and intuitive part of your journey.

So, as you explore the path of self-discovery and growth, let self-compassion be a constant companion. Let it comfort you in times of difficulty and gently encourage you to move forward.

Celebrating Progress

As you continue to walk the journey of self-discovery and growth through your Somatic Yoga practices, it's essential to take time to celebrate your progress and the transformative work you're doing. Acknowledging your achievements, no matter how small they may seem, is a powerful way to reinforce your commitment to mind-body wellness and cultivate a sense of joy and gratitude along the path.

You will perhaps notice that you're able to hold a challenging pose with greater ease and stability than before, or that your breathing remains steady and calm even in moments of intensity. Maybe you find yourself responding to stress or difficult emotions with greater patience and equanimity, or you sense a newfound feeling of connection and aliveness in your body. These moments of progress, however fleeting or understated, are all signs that your practice is working. They are evidence of the seeds of change taking root within you, the subtle shifts in your being that are laying the foundation for greater health, happiness, and wholeness. But celebrating your progress doesn't have to be a grand or elaborate affair. It can be as simple as taking a moment after your practice to close your eyes, place a hand on your heart, and offer yourself a word of appreciation or praise. It can mean writing a note of gratitude in your journal or sharing your achievements with a trusted friend or loved one.

However, you might also choose to mark significant milestones or breakthroughs with something special, such as taking a relaxing bath, booking a massage, or treating yourself to a nice meal. The key is to find ways to celebrate your journey that are meaningful to you. As you learn to celebrate your progress, because for many it is something that needs to be learned, with a sense of joy and reverence, you begin to appreciate the journey you've taken on more. You start to recognize that every moment of your practice—every breath and every movement—is an opportunity to connect with your own self and to move closer to the truth of who you are.

It also keeps you motivated and engaged in the practice, even on those days when you may feel challenged or simply discouraged. It's focusing on the positive things that allow for a good change, and in this case, celebrating your progress is certainly something positive.

Resources for Ongoing Support

Having access to a variety of supportive resources can be incredibly valuable for deepening your practice, expanding your knowledge, and staying inspired along the path. Whether you're looking to explore new techniques, gain insights from experienced teachers, or connect with like-minded communities, there is a wealth of information available to support your ongoing growth and development. A great way to increase your understanding and enrich your practice is through reading and joining communities as well as workshops.

Online Communities and Workshops

One of the most powerful ways to stay inspired, motivated, and supported on your Somatic Yoga journey is by connecting with like-minded individuals who share your passion for well-being. In today's digital age, there are numerous online communities and workshops that offer opportunities to deepen your practice, learn from experienced teachers, and cultivate meaningful relationships with fellow practitioners from around the world. Participating in online forums and social media groups dedicated to somatic yoga and mindfulness can be a wonderful way to exchange ideas, ask questions, and receive guidance from knowledgeable and supportive community members. These virtual spaces often feature lively discussions on a wide range of topics, from specific yoga techniques and meditation practices to the latest research and insights in the field of mind-body wellness.

Some popular online communities to explore include:

1 Somatic Experience:

- Mindful Teachers Hub
- Trauma-Informed and Community Yoga Teachers
- Embodiment Open

2 Reddit Subreddits:

- r/yoga
- r/meditation
- r/traumatoolbox

3 Online Forums:

- Yoga Journal
- Somatic Experiencing Practitioners Directory
- The Institute for Meditation and Psychotherapy

In addition to online forums and social media groups, attending virtual workshops and webinars can be a fantastic way to further understand specific aspects of somatic yoga and mind-body wellness. Many experienced teachers and practitioners offer online classes, workshops, and immersive training programs that allow you to learn from the comfort of your own home while still benefiting from the energy and connection of a group setting.

Some notable online workshops and training providers include:

1. Embodied Philosophy: https://www.embodiedphilosophy.com/
2. The Minded Institute: https://themindedinstitute.com/
3. Yoga International: https://yogainternational.com/
4. Sounds True: https://www.soundstrue.com/
5. The Breathing Project: https://thebreathingproject.org/

When exploring online communities and workshops, remember to trust your instincts and choose spaces that feel like you belong, are welcoming, and are aligned with your values and goals. Take time to read through past discussions, familiarize yourself with the group's guidelines and culture, and participate in a way that feels genuine and nourishing to you. As you connect with others, remember that each person's journey is unique and deeply personal. Approach your interactions with a sense of openness, curiosity, and non-judgment, since there's a diverse range of experiences and perspectives that each individual brings to the community. By engaging with online communities and workshops, you not only gain access to a wealth of knowledge and support, but you also contribute to the collective knowledge and evolution of the field. Your insights, questions, and experiences have the power to enrich and inspire others, creating a ripple effect of positive transformation in the world.

Local Resources

While online communities and resources offer a wealth of support for your Somatic Yoga journey, there is something uniquely powerful about connecting with others in person, in your local community. Seeking out nearby yoga studios, wellness centers, and meditation groups can provide you with amazing opportunities for deepening your practice, receiving personalized guidance, and growing meaningful relationships with fellow practitioners in your area. One of the great benefits of exploring local resources is the ability to experience the connection of practicing in a shared physical space. When you attend a somatic yoga class or meditation group in person, you have the opportunity to immerse yourself fully in the experience, free from the distractions and limitations of digital screens and remote interactions.

In a live-class setting, you can receive hands-on adjustments and personalized modifications from skilled teachers who can observe your unique body and offer guidance tailored to your specific needs and goals. You can also benefit from the collective energy and intention of practicing alongside others and having that sense of shared purpose and mutual support.

To find local resources that might be of your interests and needs, consider the following strategies:

1. Search online directories and review sites, such as Yelp, Google Maps, or MindBody, for yoga studios, wellness centers, and meditation groups in your area. Read reviews and descriptions to get a sense of each space's approach,

philosophy, and offerings.

2. Ask for recommendations from friends, family members, or colleagues who share your interest in mind-body wellness. Personal referrals can be a great way to find trusted, reputable resources that align with your values and goals.

3. Check local event listings, community bulletins, or holistic health publications for workshops, classes, or special events related to Somatic Yoga and embodied mindfulness. These can be wonderful opportunities to explore new practices, connect with local teachers, and meet like-minded individuals in your community.

4. Visit the websites or social media pages of local yoga studios, wellness centers, and meditation groups to learn more about their class schedules, teacher bios, and special offerings. Many spaces offer introductory deals or trial periods that allow you to experience their services before committing to a longer-term membership or package.

When exploring local resources, remember to be open and willing to step outside your comfort zone. Trying out a new studio or attending a class with an unfamiliar teacher can be intimidating at first, but it can also lead to incredible breakthroughs and discoveries in your practice. As you connect with local teachers and practitioners, don't hesitate to ask questions, share your goals and challenges, and seek out guidance and support when needed. Remember, once again, that your somatic yoga journey is a deeply personal and evolving process, and the right resources and relationships can make all the difference in helping you navigate the path with greater ease, joy, and fulfillment.

Ultimately, by combining online resources with the intimacy and connection of local, in-person experiences, you create a rich and dynamic ecosystem of support for your ongoing growth and transformation. You tap into the knowledge of a global community while also anchoring your practice in the grounded reality of your local environment.

As we come to the close of this chapter on your future with somatic yoga, take a moment to reflect on the incredible journey that lies ahead. Throughout these pages, we've explored the vast potential of this practice, not just as a means of improving physical health and vitality but as a pathway to deeper self-discovery. We began by emphasizing the importance of setting clear intentions and goals for your ongoing practice, recognizing that a strong sense of purpose and direction can be powerful in guiding you in your path. By taking time to reflect on your deepest aspirations and values, you lay the foundation for your journey. From there, we explored the value of creating a personalized wellness plan, one that integrates Somatic Yoga with other mind-body practices, self-care practices, and support systems that help you on every level. We emphasized the importance of improving self-compassion and celebrating your progress along the way. Recognizing that the journey of Somatic Yoga is non-linear and deeply personal you should embrace your experience with kindness, patience, and trust in your own development.

To support you in your ongoing exploration, I provided you with a wealth of resources and recommendations, from inspiring books and articles to online communities, workshops, and local studios and teachers (or a way to find them). Ultimately, what I want to transmit with this chapter is empowerment, possibility, and profound trust in your journey ahead. If you align your Somatic Yoga practice with your deepest intentions, create a supportive environment for your progress, and stay open to the wisdom and guidance that arise along the way, you set yourself up for a future of ever-greater health, happiness, and self-realization.

As you continue to go through this path with courage, dedication, and an open heart, know that you are not alone. You are part of a global community of practitioners, all committed to the same vision of healing, wholeness, and awakening. Together, we are creating a new paradigm of well-being—one breath, one movement, one moment at a time.

So before you turn the page on this chapter, I want you to take a moment to pause, to place a hand on your heart, and to express a profound sense of gratitude and appreciation for yourself and your own being. Thank yourself for the dedication and discipline that you've brought to your practice and for showing up on your mat day after day, even when it felt challenging or uncomfortable. Remember the strength and resilience that you've developed, not just in your physical body but in your mental and emotional state as well. Express gratitude for the moments of breakthrough and revelation that you've experienced and for the insights and epiphanies that have shifted your perspective and opened up new possibilities for your life. Celebrate the times when you've been able to meet yourself with kindness and compassion, even in the face of difficulty or self-doubt.

Acknowledge the profound gift that you've given yourself by prioritizing your own healing and growth and by investing in your own holistic well-being and self-discovery. Understand that by showing up for yourself in this way, you are not only changing your own life, but you are also contributing to the healing and awakening of the world around you. As you offer yourself this heartfelt expression of gratitude, allow yourself to really feel the truth of your worth, as well as the incredible value and beauty of your existence. Let this moment of self-recognition be a powerful affirmation of your commitment to your unfolding and a reminder of the importance and significance of your journey. And know that the work that you're doing—the seeds that you're planting through your Somatic Yoga practice—is not just for your benefit but for the benefit of all beings everywhere.

Conclusion

As we come to the close of this exploration into the world of Somatic Yoga, let us take a moment to reflect on the incredible journey that we've undertaken together. Throughout the pages of this book, we've analyzed the depths of our being, uncovering the profound knowledge and potential that lie within our own experience.

We started with an understanding of somatic therapy and its power to heal and change as we set the foundation for a journey of self-discovery. We learned that by tuning into the sensations and messages of our body, we can access a deep well of insight and resilience that can guide us toward greater health, wholeness, and vitality. From there, we explored the importance of shorter focus sessions, understanding that even brief moments of embodied presence can have a profound impact on our well-being. We discovered that by bringing mindful attention to our breath and our body, even amid our busy lives, we can develop a greater sense of calm, clarity, and connection.

As we took a deep dive into the practice of somatic breathwork, we learned to harness the power of our breath as a tool for self-regulation and change within ourselves. And by exploring various breathing techniques and their effects on our nervous system, we found a powerful pathway to inner peace, balance, and vitality. Moving into Somatic Yoga poses, we experienced firsthand the shifting power of movement. These practices are designed to release emotional blockages, alleviate stress and tension, and promote strength and flexibility, allowing us to discover a new level of freedom, resilience, and ease within ourselves.

We also explored the relationship between Somatic Yoga and weight loss and understood that true change arises not through force or deprivation, but through a loving and compassionate approach to our own wholeness. We can reach that by connecting with our body's innate wisdom and needs, as we learn to nourish ourselves from the inside out. The culmination of our journey brought us to the 21-Day Somatic

Evolution, a powerful invitation to commit to our own growth and transformation in a deep yet sustained way. Through daily practices, reflections, and insights, we discovered the incredible potential that lies within consistent, dedicated practice and the ways in which small, daily steps can lead to profound shifts in our lives.

In the last chapter, we turned towards the future, envisioning a life mingled with the knowledge and practices of Somatic Yoga. We explored the importance of setting intentions, developing a personal practice, and developing a supportive community of fellow travelers on the path. We recognized that the journey of awakening is a lifelong one, full of endless opportunities for growth, discovery, and transformation.

As we close this book and prepare to step forward into the next phase of our journey, let us take a moment to celebrate the incredible work that we've done. Through our willingness to show up fully, to embrace the discomfort and vulnerability of growth, and to trust in the understanding of our own experience, we have planted the seeds for a life of incredible richness, meaning, and purpose. I hope the lessons and insights that we've gained through this exploration continue to guide and inspire you, both on and off the mat. May you continue to develop a deep sense of presence, compassion, and loving awareness in all that you do, and may we trust in the profound intelligence and resilience that lie within our own being.

Take a moment to reflect on where you were when you first began this journey and where you are now. Notice the shifts, both subtle and profound, that have taken place within your body, mind, and spirit. Perhaps you've experienced a greater sense of ease and freedom in your physical movements or a deeper sense of calm and centeredness in your mental and emotional beings. Or maybe you've tapped into a well of inner strength and resilience that you never knew existed, or have developed a more loving and compassionate relationship with yourself and others. Wherever your journey has taken you, know that every step that you've taken and every moment of presence and awareness that you brought to your practice has been a powerful act of self-love and self-care. You chose to prioritize your own growth and well-being, so you've not only changed your own life but also contributed to others around you.

So keep showing up, keep exploring, and keep celebrating your progress along the way. By trusting in your own journey of growth and change, you are moving forward. And know that you are not alone but are part of a global community of practitioners and seekers, all committed to the same vision of wholeness, connection, and awakening. Together, we are co-creating a world of greater peace, compassion, and understanding, one breath and one moment at a time.

As you continue on this path, I encourage you to stay open and curious, to approach each moment with a beginner's mind and a willingness to learn and grow. Remember that the practices of somatic yoga are not static or fixed but are alive and evolving, just like you. So keep exploring, keep experimenting, and keep discovering new ways to deepen your connection to yourself and to the world around you. Stay committed to your daily practice, even if it's just for a few minutes each day. Trust that by showing up consistently and wholeheartedly, you are creating a powerful momentum of change that will ripple out into all the other areas of your being. And when challenges or obstacles arise, as they certainly will, remember to meet yourself with kindness, compassion, and understanding, knowing that each moment is an opportunity to begin again to recommit to your own progress.

Seek out opportunities to connect with others who share your passion for growth, whether it's through local classes and workshops, online communities, or personal relationships. Remember that we are all in this together and that by supporting and uplifting one another, we create a powerful force for healing and transformation. So go forth with courage, compassion, and an open heart, trusting that the journey ahead is full of endless opportunities for growth and discovery. May the practices of Somatic Yoga continue to guide and support you, now and always, as you navigate the ever-unfolding path of your own becoming.

Before we part ways, I want to take a moment to express my deepest appreciation for your presence, your engagement, and your willingness to show up fully for this journey of Somatic Yoga. Your dedication, your curiosity, and your openness to growth and transformation have been a true inspiration, and I feel honored to have been a part of your path. I want to invite you to reflect honestly and authentically on your experience with this book. Your feedback, insights, and reflections are a precious gift, not only to me as the author but to the larger community of practitioners and seekers who may benefit from your wisdom and perspective.

So I ask you, with an open heart and a sincere desire to learn and grow, to take a moment to share your honest review of this book. What resonated with you most deeply? What challenged you or pushed you out of your comfort zone? What insights or aha moments did you have along the way? And what, if anything, do you feel could be improved or expanded upon in future editions? Please know that there are no right or wrong answers here and that every piece of feedback is valuable and appreciated. Whether you choose to share your reflections publicly or privately, know that your voice matters and that by sharing your experience, you are contributing to the collective progress of this transformative practice.

So thank you, once again, for your presence, your practice, and your willingness to show up fully for your own growth. And thank you for being a part of this incredible community of practitioners, all committed to the same vision of wholeness and connection.

Exercise List

Deep Hip Stretch 19

Supine Glute Stretch 20

Reverse Lunge Reach 21

Deep Neck Stretch 22

Kneeling Turn and Reach 23

Forward Fold (Uttanasana) 27

Child's Pose (Balasana) 29

Heart-Opening Pose 30

Cat-Cow Pose (Marjaryasana-Bitilasana) 31

Pigeon Pose (Eka Pada Rajakapotasana) 33

Bridge Pose (Setu Bandhasana) 34

Reclining Bound Angle Pose (Supta Baddha Konasana) 35

Twisting Chair Pose (Parivrtta Utkatasana) 36

Seated Forward Fold (Paschimottanasana) 37

Corpse Pose (Savasana) 38

Seated Neck Release 44

Shoulder Rolls 45

Thread the Needle Pose (Parsva Balasana) 46

Extended Puppy Pose (Uttana Shishosana) 47

Supported Fish Pose 48

Supine Twist (Supta Matsyendrasana) 49

Sphinx Pose (Salamba Bhujangasana) 50

Standing Forward Fold with Clasped Hands 51

Seated Forward Fold with Side Stretch 52

Legs Up the Wall Pose (Viparita Karani) 53

Warrior II Pose (Virabhadrasana II) 58

Chair Pose (Utkatasana) 59

Plank Pose (Phalakasana) 60

Boat Pose (Navasana) 61

Downward-Facing Dog (Adho Mukha Svanasana) 62

Extended Triangle Pose (Utthita Trikonasana) 63

Side Plank Pose (Vasisthasana) 64

Low Lunge (Anjaneyasana) 65

Crow Pose (Bakasana) 66

Supported Shoulder Pose 67

Mountain Pose (Tadasana) 73

Locust Pose (Salabhasana) 74

Extended Side Angle Pose (Utthita Parsvakonasana) 75

Wide-Legged Forward (Prasarita Padottanasana) 76

Warrior III Pose (Virabhadrasana III) 77

Dolphin Plank Pose 78

Firefly Pose (Tittibhasana) 79

Half Moon (Ardha Chandrasana) 80

Revolved Triangle Pose (Parivrtta Trikonasana) 81

Camel Pose (Ustrasana) 82

Up-Dog Stretch 83

Spinal Roll Stretch 85

Armpit Stretch 86

Chest Stretch 87

Butterfly Stretch 88

Made in United States
North Haven, CT
15 August 2024